Walter Robson

Medieval Britain

Oxford University Press

Oxford University Press, Walton Street, Oxford OX2 6DP

Oxford New York Toronto
Delhi Bombay Calcutta Madras Karachi
Petaling Jaya Singapore Hong Kong Tokyo
Nairobi Dar es Salaam Cape Town

and associated companies in

Berlin Ibadan

Oxford is a trade mark of Oxford University Press

First published 1991
Reprinted 1992
ISBN 0 19 833545 8

Typeset by Pentacor PLC, High Wycombe, Bucks
Printed in Italy
by G. Canale & C. S.p.A. - Borgaro T.se - Torino

Acknowledgements

The publishers would like to thank the following for permission to reproduce photographs:

Reproduced by gracious permission of Her Majesty the Queen: p32 (right); Bibliothèque Nationale, Paris: p84 (right); The Bodleian Library, Oxford: p23, p53 (bottom), p76 (roll 172B), p77 (bottom) (Ms Bodley 764 f44), p82 (top left) (Ms 285 f6v) / Courtesy of the President and Fellows of Corpus Christi College, Oxford, p83 (bottom right), p87 (Ms Bodley 270b f129vd), p88 (bottom) (Ms Bodley 264 f105), p89 (Ms Douce 6 f22); The Bridgeman Art Library: p63 / Bibliothèque Nationale, Paris; The British Library Board: p19, p21 (Harl Roll Y 6 (3)), p24 (Sloane 2435 f44v), p25 (Roy 2a XXii f220), p32 (left) Add 4838, pp50–51 (Add 42130, f158, f173, f171, f172v, f170, f170v), p52 (Cott Tib B V f5 pt1), p56, p59 (left) (Roy 18 E I f175), p60 (left) (Cott Jul E IV f7v), p60 (right) (Add 42130 f202v), p68 (Add 40742 f10), p72 (bottom) (Roy 15 E II f265), p73 (right) (Roy 15E III f259), p75 (Egerton 1894 f5v), p77 (top), 82 (top right) (Harl 4431 f81), p83 (bottom left) (Add 28162 f10v), p84 (left) Harl 3745 f1), p95 (bottom) (Cott Tib A IV f9v); Reproduced by courtesy of the Trustees of the British Museum p40; By permission of the Duke of Buccleugh & Queensberry KT and with the approval of the Keeper of the Records of Scotland, ref no GD 55 / 174: p42 (top); The Burrell Collection, Glasgow Museums and Art Galleries: p11; Cambridge University Collection of Air Photographs: p50 (top), p55; Courtesy of the Master and Fellows of Corpus Christi College, Cambridge: p12 (top), p37 (top left); Courtesy of the Master and Fellows of Trinity College, Cambridge: p82 (bottom), p85, p86; Reproduced by permission of the Archbishop of Canterbury and the Trustees of Lambeth Palace Library: p62, p66 (top right); The National Gallery of Ireland, Dublin: p48; the National Museum of Wales: p37 (top right); The Board of Trinity College, Dublin: p46 (top & bottom); Edinburgh University Library: p43; English Heritage: p22 (bottom); E. T. Archive: p29 / Keir Collection, p91 / Honourable Society of the Inner Temple; Fine Art Photographs: p94 / Gavin Graham Gallery; Glasgow Museums and Art Galleries: p61 (left) (Reg no 39–65e); Sonia Halliday Photographs: p17 (top), p26 (top), p26 (bottom right) / Bibliothèque Nationale, Paris, p39, p59 (right), p67; Michael Holford: p5, pp8–9, p10, p12 (bottom), p15, 17 (bottom), p33, p73 (left), p83 (top); The Museum of London: p18, p72 (top); Mary Evans Picture Library: p78, p93; National Portrait Gallery, London: p69 (left); The Pierpont Morgan Library, New York: p26 (bottom left); Royal Commission on the Historical Monuments of England: p53 (top); Historic Buildings and Monuments of Scotland: Crown copyright: p42 (bottom); Edwin Smith: 69 (right); Stiftsbibliothek St Galien, Switzerland: p49; Wales Tourist Board: p35; Reproduced by permission of the Trustees of the Wallace Collection: p61 (right); Weidenfeld & Nicolson Archives: p22 (top right) / Trinity College, Cambridge, p27 / Bibliothèque Nationale, Paris, p34, p90 / Victoria & Albert Museum, p92 / Public Record Office, London; The Welsh Folk Museum: p58 (left and right); Woodmansterne Picture Library: p16 (left & right), p22 (top left), p80, p81; ZEFA: p37 (bottom), p45; In a private collection: p44

The illustrations are by Peter Kent, Anthony Knill, Miller Craig and Cocking, Duncan Storr and Brian Walker.

Cover photograph: The capture of Jerusalem in AD 1187 by Saladin. Reproduced by kind permission of the Scala, Florence.

Contents

Preface

The title of this series is *Access to History*, and accessibility is its keynote – accessibility to National Curriculum History, in terms of both Programmes of Study and Attainment Targets.

The exercises, which refer to the text, sources, and illustrations, are intended to extend factual knowledge, promote comprehension, and develop a range of skills, all consistent with National Curriculum Attainment Targets. The "criteria grid" (at the end of the book) shows how the individual exercises relate to the Attainment Targets.

It is not expected that pupils will work through the book unaided. Teachers will wish to omit some exercises and amend others. They will probably decide that some exercises which are set for individual work would be tackled more successfully by using a group or class approach, with the teacher him / herself as leader. The book's aim is to provide teachers with a useful set of resources, not to usurp their role.

Pages marked with the symbol may be photocopied at will, free from copyright. Teachers may wish to use this facility to hasten pupils' progress (e.g. they could write answers on the photocopied pages), or to set homework assignments, or to economise on resources.

The Norman Conquest

A The Battle of Hastings

A south wind blew in the English Channel on 28 September 1066. It took a fleet of little ships across the sea from France to England. They were packed with knights, archers, and horses. **Duke William of Normandy** was on his way to England.

King Harold of England was waiting with his army in Sussex (look at the map). But he heard that the king of Norway, had invaded the north of England. Harold marched his men north at once, and beat the Norwegians in a battle near York.

While Harold was in the north, Duke William and his army landed in Sussex. As soon as Harold heard the news, he rushed south again. But he moved too fast for some of his men. He reached Sussex with only half the army.

The English and Normans met in battle near Hastings, on 14 October 1066. It was a long, hard fight, which the Normans won. By the end of the day, Harold and all his bodyguard lay dead. Just two months later, William was crowned king of England. We now call him **William the Conqueror**.

Now try Exercise 1.1.

England in 1066

--→ Route of Norwegian Invaders
→ Route of Norman Invaders
✕ Battles

Exercise 1.1

Read **Section A** and look at the map. Fill in the spaces in the sentences. Choose one of the answers in brackets.

a William was duke of _____
   (Sussex/Brittany/Normandy)

b William crossed the Channel because he wanted to be king of _____ (England/Norway/France)

c The king of England was called _____
   (Harold/Edward/Henry)

d Harold marched north to fight _____
   (the king of Scotland/the king of Norway/some Yorkshire rebels)

e The English and Normans fought a battle near _____
   _____ (London/Hastings/York)

B The Normans take control

The English did not want a Norman king. There were revolts, but William crushed them. Men who fought against the Normans were killed, and so were their wives and children. The Normans pulled down their homes and set fire to their crops.

The Normans built castles in all the main towns and in many villages. Castles were places where the new Norman lords could live in safety. And it was from the castles that Norman knights rode out to punish the English when there was trouble.

At first, they built **motte-and-bailey** castles. The bailey was a mound of earth, protected by a ditch and a wooden stockade, with wooden huts inside. This is where the Normans normally lived. If the English attacked, and broke into the bailey, they would retreat to the motte, a higher mound, with a wooden tower on top. (Look at the drawing below.)

After a few years, the Normans began to build stone castles. Instead of a wooden tower, they built a keep. This was a high stone tower with thick walls – so strong that many keeps are still standing. (Look at the photograph below.)

Now try Exercise 1.2.

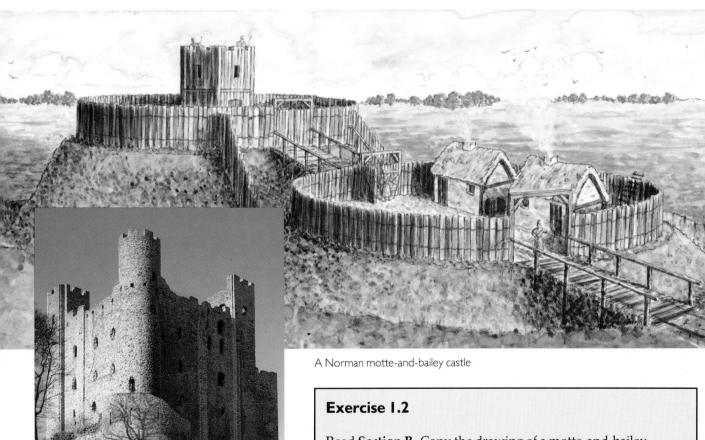

A Norman motte-and-bailey castle

Rochester Castle in Kent. The stone keep was built in 1130. The walls are nearly 4 metres thick.

Exercise 1.2

Read **Section B**. Copy the drawing of a motte-and-bailey castle. Add labels, using words from this list:

bailey   stockade   ditch   bridge   tower   motte   huts.

C Who owns the land?

William the Conqueror said that all the land in England belonged to him. He kept some of it for himself and he gave some to his lords. They became William's **barons** (another word for lords). The most important barons were called **earls**.

The barons and earls were the leaders of the king's army. They had helped him to conquer England, and now they helped him to rule it. The chief men in the church – the bishops and abbots – were just as important as the barons and earls. They too were given land by the king.

Each baron, earl, bishop and abbot paid rent for his land, not with money, but with help in time of war. He promised to lead his **knights** into battle on the king's side whenever there was a war. The more land he had, the more knights he had to bring. We call this the **feudal system**.

The lords and bishops who paid their rent to the king are known as **tenants-in-chief**. When they got their land, they had to kneel before their king and promise to serve him. This was called **doing homage** to the king. A man who did homage to the king was the king's **vassal**.

William did not always trust his great lords. He knew that if the king was not strong, they might rebel. So in 1086 he decided to find out how much land each of them had. He sent his men to each county in England. They had to find out who owned the land, and how much it was worth. They wrote their report in what we call **Domesday Book**.

Now try Exercise 1.3.

THE FEUDAL SYSTEM IN ENGLAND

THE KING

TENANTS-IN-CHIEF
(VASSALS OF THE KING)

EARL OF DERBY
(Paid rent for his land with 80 knights)

ABBOT OF WESTMINSTER
(Paid rent for his land with 15 knights)

MANY OTHER TENANTS-IN-CHIEF

THE MORE LAND A TENANT-IN-CHIEF HAD, THE MORE KNIGHTS HE HAD TO SEND TO SERVE THE KING

Sources

We find out about the past from **sources**. Books and papers are **written sources**. Books written by monks soon after 1066 tell the story of the Norman Conquest. The monks were not present at the battle of Hastings, but some of them may have talked to men who were there. **Source 1b** and **Source 1c** are from books written by these monks.

Old coins, buildings, weapons, and pictures are also **sources**. The Bayeux Tapestry (**Sources 1d to 1i**) tells the story of the Norman invasion in pictures.

Source 1a

King William sent his men to all parts of England. They had to find out how much land the king had. They also found out how much land the churches and his barons held. This was done so well that every scrap of land, and every ox, cow, and pig was put into the report.

Written by a monk at Worcester soon after the year 1100.

Exercise 1.3

Read **Section** C, then answer the questions in sentences.

a What were barons?
b What were earls?
c In the feudal system, great men paid rent for their land with what?
d What were tenants-in-chief?
e What did doing homage mean?
f What was a vassal?
g What was Domesday Book? (Read **Source 1a**.)

Source 1b

William built three thousand ships, and filled them with mighty horses and brave men. He crossed the sea and landed at Pevensey. He left some of his troops there, and hurried on to Hastings with the rest. He built a castle there. Harold rode all night to reach the enemy. The battle began at nine o'clock, and went on all day. Harold fought in the front rank of the army, and he fell, covered with wounds.

Written by a monk called Robert at a monastery in Normandy, about four years after the Battle of Hastings.

Source 1c

The Normans attacked before Harold's army was ready. The English fought hard, and many men were killed on both sides. King Harold was killed, and so were his brothers Leofwine and Gyrth.

Taken from an old book called the *Anglo-Saxon Chronicle*. This part was possibly written by a monk in York shortly after 1066.

Exercise 1.4

Read the notes on **Sources**. Read **Sources 1b** and **1c**, and look at **Sources 1d** to **1i** on pages 8–9. Now try the questions.

a Who wrote **Source 1b**, and when?
b **Source 1c** comes from which old book?
c Who wrote **Source 1c**, and when?
d Were the authors of **Sources 1b** and **1c** at the battle of Hastings?
e What are **Sources 1d** to **1i** taken from?
f Who made the Bayeux Tapestry, and when?

Sources 1d – 1i   The Bayeux Tapestry

The Bayeux Tapestry is a piece of embroidered linen, about 70 metres long. It tells a story in pictures, with words in Latin. It was probably made by some ladies in Canterbury not long after 1066. You can still see the tapestry in a museum in Bayeux in Normandy. Six scenes are printed for you here.

Source 1d

The Normans prepare to invade England.

Source 1e

The Normans cross the English Channel.

Source 1h

The Latin words say 'The brothers Leofwine and Gyrth are killed'.

Source 1i

The death of King Harold

Source **1f**

The Normans build a castle at Hastings.

Source **1g**

The battle of Hastings – English on the left, Normans on the right.

Exercise 1.5

Read the written sources (**Sources 1b** and **1c**) and look at the pictures in **Sources 1d** to **1i**. Read the notes with **Sources 1d** to **1i** too. Now try the questions. Answer them in sentences.

a What are the men doing in **Source 1d**?
b One of the written sources tells us about William getting ready to cross the English Channel.
  i Which source?
  ii What does it say?
c i How big were the ships in **Source 1e**?
  ii How many masts and sails did they have?
  iii How were they steered?
d Which written source says the same as **Source 1f**?
e Look at **Source 1g**. How were the English and the Norman soldiers:
  i the same?
  ii different?
f **Source 1h** tells us something that is mentioned by one of the written sources.
  i What is that?
  ii Which written source does not mention it?
g i Which of the soldiers in **Source 1i** do you think is King Harold?
  ii Does **Source 1i** tell us how Harold was killed?
  iii Do the written sources tell us how Harold was killed?

Exercise 1.6

Look again at **Sources 1d** to **1i**, then tell the story in your own words. Put some of the details from the pictures into your story. (You could write out your story, or put it onto tape, or tell it to the rest of your group.)

2 Knights, Lords, and Kings

A Knights

War took up a great deal of a king's time in the Middle Ages. Earls and barons were soldiers above all. Even bishops and abbots sometimes led their knights into battle.

Knights were soldiers who fought on horseback. They were the main fighting force in every army. A knight's main weapons were the **lance** (a long, thin spear) and the sword. (Look at **Sources 1g, 1h** and **1i** on pages 8 and 9.) It took many years of training to become a skilled knight.

A knight went into battle dressed in armour made from lots of iron rings (sometimes called **chain-mail**). He had an iron helmet, and he carried a long, narrow shield. A knight had to be strong to carry all that weight. So had his horse! War-horses were big, heavy animals. They could trot, but not gallop.

At first, Norman knights lived in the great lords' castles. But not long after 1066, the lords began to give away pieces of land to their knights. A knight paid rent for his land by doing guard duty at his lord's castle, and serving with his lord in the army.

Now try Exercise 2.1.

Source 2a

This scene from the Bayeux Tapestry shows the Normans getting ready to invade England. The Latin words say: 'These men are carrying arms'.

Exercise 2.1

Read **Section A**, and look at **Sources 2a** and **2b**. Answer questions **a** to **e** in sentences.

a Which weapons can you see in **Source 2a**?

b How are the men in **Source 2a** carrying the suits of armour? Why do you think they are carrying them like that?

c Describe the helmets worn by the knights in **Source 2b**.

d Describe the shields carried by the knights in **Source 2b**.

e What does **Source 2b** tell us about what knights wore under their armour?

f Draw a picture of a Norman knight. Put labels on your drawing to show the names of his weapons and pieces of equipment.

Source 2b

A bronze carving showing three Norman knights

Here's the pear you asked for.

Idiot! J'ai demandé mon père.

For 200 years after 1066, all of England's rulers spoke French. Kings, earls, barons, and bishops were French. They knew enough English to give orders to their servants, but no more. "Old English", as we call it, was the language of the peasants. But there were far more peasants than lords. In time, English took over, and by the year 1400 everyone spoke it. By then, though, it was a mixture of "Old English" and the French the Normans brought to England.

B Civil war

Like most countries in the Middle Ages, England was a **monarchy** – it was ruled by a king. And the king needed to be strong. But not all kings were strong enough. King **Stephen**, William I's grandson, spent most of his reign fighting a **civil war** against his cousin **Matilda**.

The earls and barons had their own castles and armies of knights and archers. In Stephen's reign, some fought for the king, and some fought for Matilda. Most of the time, they did as they liked. The worst of them robbed and tortured the English peasants and burned their homes.

When Stephen died, **Henry II**, Matilda's son, became king. Henry was only 21 years old. He was good-looking, tough, and fond of sport. He was also a wise and brave ruler. He was not afraid of the great lords, and had made up his mind that there would be no more civil war.

When he was in England, Henry travelled far and wide, making sure that there was peace, law, and order in the land. He sent his judges round the country, so that accused persons would get a proper trial. He made all the lords and knights swear to obey him, their king.

Now try Exercise 2.2.

Attacking a castle: a knight urges on the footsoldiers. The picture was drawn in about 1250.

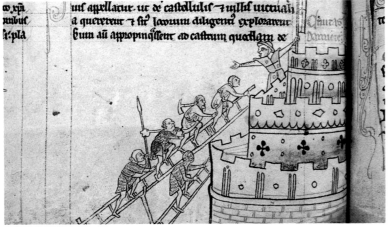

Exercise 2.2

Read **Section B**. Some passages from the *Anglo-Saxon Chronicle* have been printed below, in the wrong order. Write them out in the proper order (earliest first).

1100 William II was killed by an arrow fired by one of his men when he was out hunting.

1137 All the great men built castles and refused to obey King Stephen.

1068 William I built a castle at Nottingham and two castles at York.

1120 Henry I's son was drowned when his ship was wrecked in the Channel.

1154 Stephen died. Henry II arrived from France and was crowned king.

1131 There was a terrible outbreak of disease among cattle and pigs.

1092 King William II made many peasants take their wives and animals and go and live in Cumberland.

The castle of Angers, one of Henry II's strongholds in France

C Henry II's empire

Before he became king of England in 1154, Henry II already ruled part of France. Henry's father was Geoffrey, the count of **Anjou** and **Maine**. (Look at the map on page 13.) Like most great lords, he spent much of his time at war. In 1150, Geoffrey conquered **Normandy**, and gave it to Henry. When Geoffrey died in 1151, Henry got Anjou and Maine.

Henry's wife, **Eleanor**, brought him **Aquitaine** as well. Eleanor was the **heiress** of the duke of Aquitaine. This meant that she was the only daughter of the last duke, and that he had no sons. When he died, all the duke's land (most of south-west France) went to Eleanor's husband.

Later, Henry's third son, another **Geoffrey**, married the heiress of the duke of **Brittany**. So Brittany came under Henry's rule also. By 1171, Henry II was master of half of France. The French king wanted to drive him out. So Henry had to spend most of his time in France, fighting or getting ready for war.

Now try Exercise 2.3.

Henry II's Empire

Lands controlled by Henry II

Lands controlled by the King of France

Norman knights won control of parts of South Wales in William the Conqueror's time.

Henry II made himself ruler of part of Ireland in 1171.

Exercise 2.3

Read **Section C**, and look at the map. Complete the following table.

Place	How and when Henry II got control
England	Henry became king in _____ when Stephen died.
Normandy	Henry's father conquered Normandy. Henry became duke in _____.
Anjou and Maine	Henry got these counties when his _____ died in 1151.
Aquitaine	Henry's wife, _____, was the heiress. She was the _____ of the last _____ of Aquitaine.
Brittany	Henry's son _____ married the _____ of the duke of Brittany.
Wales	Part of _____ Wales was conquered by the _____ _____.
Ireland	Henry became ruler of part of Ireland in _____.

Source 2c

When Stephen was king, the great lords built castles everywhere, without the king's permission. Then they seized the men and women who had some money. They tortured them to make them hand over their gold and silver. Some were hung up by their thumbs, and others were put in pits full of snakes. The lords made the peasants pay them taxes as well. When the peasants had no more to give, the lords burned their homes.

From the *Anglo-Saxon Chronicle*. This part was written by a monk at Peterborough in about 1155.

Source 2d

When Stephen died, Henry II became king. Straight away, he said that lords who had built castles in Stephen's reign had to pull them down. Henry was keen on law and order. He sent judges round England to keep the wicked lords in check, and to see that all men got justice. For this, Henry won the praise and thanks of his people.

From *The History of England*, written by a monk called William of Newburgh at a monastery in Yorkshire in about 1190.

Exercise 2.4

Read **Sources 2c** and **2d** and read the note on fact and opinion.

a Write down *three* facts from **Source 2c**.
b What were the opinions of the author of **Source 2c** on:
   i King Stephen?
   ii the great lords?
c Write down *three* facts from **Source 2d**.
d What was the author's opinion of Henry II?
e What was the common people's opinion of Henry II?
f What would be the great lords' opinion of Henry II?
g Why would the common people and the great lords have different opinions?

Fact and opinion

A **fact** is something which is, or was, true. It is a **fact** that the Normans conquered England.

An **opinion** is what someone thinks or thought. The English people's **opinion** was that the Normans were cruel and greedy.

Exercise 2.5

Look at the cartoon on page 11 and read the caption. Some of the words we now use come from Old English and some from French.
These words are from Old English:

Bloom, Bowman, Folk, Hunt, Leave, Old, Pretty, Right, Teach.

These words come from French:

Archer, Ancient, Beautiful, Chase, Correct, Depart, Flower, Instruct, People.

Find the pairs of words, one English, one French, with the same meanings. Write them out in a chart.

3 The Church

A The village church

Most people in western Europe belonged to the **Roman Catholic** church in the Middle Ages. The church was at the centre of everything that went on. Babies were baptised by the priest in the church. Young couples were married at the church door. The dead were buried in the church yard. People were supposed to go to **Mass** (the church service) on Sundays and the main "holy days". These were the only days off work that they got.

All men and women believed in Heaven and Hell. Rich people left land and money to the church in their wills because they hoped it would help them get into Heaven. The church used the money to look after the old and sick.

Village priests were simple men. They could usually just manage to read, and knew enough **Latin** to say the Mass. Priests were not supposed to marry, but a lot of them did have wives. Most priests must have looked and talked like the peasants around them.

Now try Exercise 3.1.

The front of the twelfth-century church at Iffley in Oxfordshire

Source 3a

He has been a parish priest for more than 30 years, but he can neither sing the Mass properly, nor read the Bible. He can't explain the psalms to the people. But he's good at hunting hares in the fields.

From *Piers Ploughman*, a poem written by William Langland in about 1380.

Source 3b

The parson was a poor man. But he knew the Bible and could preach it to the people. He did not like taking money from poor men, and would often give away his own money.

From *The Canterbury Tales* by Geoffrey Chaucer – see Source 3f.

Fact or fiction?

Sources 3a and **3b** are **fiction**, not fact – these are **not about real** priests. But there must have been a lot of priests just like these two in the Middle Ages.

Exercise 3.1

Read **Section A** and **Sources 3a** and **3b**. Answer the questions in sentences.

a Who wrote **Source 3a**, and when?
b Who wrote **Source 3b**, and when?
c Are **Sources 3a** and **3b** fact or fiction?
d Why are **Sources 3a** and **3b** useful to the student of history?
e What were the differences between the priests in **Sources 3a** and **3b**?

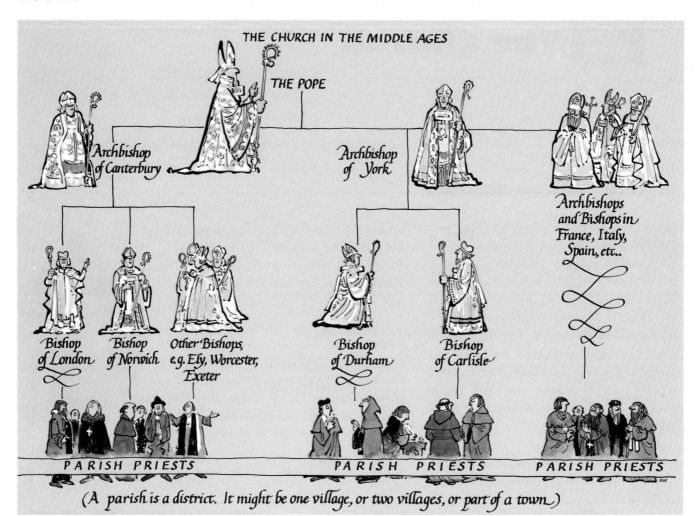

THE CHURCH IN THE MIDDLE AGES

THE POPE

Archbishop of Canterbury

Archbishop of York

Archbishops and Bishops in France, Italy, Spain, etc...

Bishop of London

Bishop of Norwich

Other Bishops, e.g. Ely, Worcester, Exeter

Bishop of Durham

Bishop of Carlisle

PARISH PRIESTS   PARISH PRIESTS   PARISH PRIESTS

(A parish is a district. It might be one village, or two villages, or part of a town.)

Source 3c

Durham Cathedral. This part of the cathedral was built in the twelfth century. (Norman style)

Source 3d

Exeter Cathedral. This part of the cathedral was built in the fourteenth century. (Decorated style)

B **Bishops and cathedrals**

The head of the Catholic church was the **Pope**, who lived in Rome. Each **see** (or district) was under the control of a **bishop**. Bishops had to make sure that the priests in their sees could read, and that they said Mass at the right times. Bishops took orders from **archbishops**. The Archbishops of Canterbury and York were the top men in the church in England.

The king picked most of the bishops. He often gave the jobs to his own advisers and friends. Many bishops stayed with the king at court. Some never went near their sees.

The chief church in each see was the **cathedral**. The cathedrals built in the Middle Ages are some of the finest buildings in England. The cathedrals were bright and colourful inside. The walls were painted, and there were lots of sculptures, and gold and silver ornaments.

Now try Exercise 3.2.

This stained-glass window in Canterbury Cathedral shows pilgrims at the tomb of St Thomas (page 18).

Centuries

A **century** is a period of a hundred years.
The **first century** A.D. was the hundred years from AD 1 to AD 100.
The **second century** A.D. was the hundred years from AD101 to AD 200.
The **seventh century** was the hundred years from AD 601 to AD 700.
The year AD 410 was in the **fifth century**.
The year AD 1359 was in the **fourteenth century**.

Source 3e

Winchester Cathedral. This part of the cathedral was built in the fifteenth century. (Perpendicular style)

Exercise 3.2

Read the note on **Centuries**, then look at **Sources 3c, 3d** and **3e**.

a Fill in the gaps in the sentences.

   i **Source 3c** is called the _____ style. It was built in the _____ century (between the years _____ and _____).

   ii **Source 3d** is called the _____ style. It was built in the _____ century (between the years _____ and _____).

   iii **Source 3e** is called the _____ style. It was built in the _____ century (between the years _____ and _____).

b Draw a time-line, from the twelfth century to the fifteenth century. Mark these styles of building against the right centuries: Norman, Decorated, Perpendicular.

C Thomas Becket

In the Middle Ages many people went on **pilgrimages**. A pilgrimage was a journey to a **shrine**. And a shrine was the place where a saint was buried, or where some holy object was kept. **Pilgrims** thought that God would be pleased with them and reward them if they travelled to a shrine and prayed there. He might cure them of their diseases, for example.

The most famous shrine in England was in Canterbury. It was the tomb of **St Thomas Becket**. Thomas was the archbishop who was murdered inside the cathedral in 1170. The pope made him a saint in 1173.

Thomas had been one of Henry II's chief advisers, and his best friend. In 1162, Henry made Thomas his Archbishop of Canterbury. He thought that Archbishop Thomas would make the church obey the king. But he was wrong. Thomas stood up to the king.

A row broke out when the king said that priests who had done wrong must be tried in the king's courts. Thomas said 'No', because the church had its own courts.

Thomas fled from England and lived in France for seven years. When he returned in 1170, the quarrel started again. So four of Henry's knights decided to do their king a good turn and get rid of his enemy. They travelled to Canterbury, and murdered Thomas in his own cathedral.

Henry took all the blame for the murder. On a summer day in 1174, the men and women of Canterbury watched him walk barefoot through their streets. When he reached the cathedral, he made the monks whip his bare back. He spent the night lying on the stone floor near Thomas's tomb.

Now try Exercise 3.3.

Source 3f

Pilgrims bought metal badges to show where they had been. The Canterbury badge, shown here, was supposed to be a flask of St Thomas's blood, which was said to cure the sick.

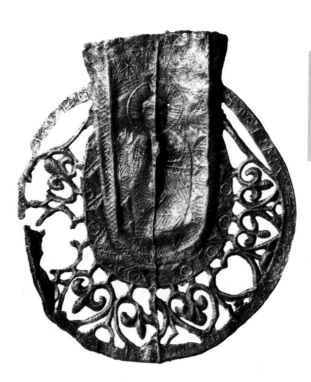

Source 3g

Some pilgrims go to the shrine of saints in far-off lands. In England, crowds go from every county to Canterbury to visit the Holy Martyr. He is famous for helping the sick.

From *The Canterbury Tales*, a long poem written by Geoffrey Chaucer in about 1390. Chaucer pretended that he was one of a group of pilgrims who travelled together from London to Canterbury. To pass the time on the journey, each of the pilgrims had to tell a story.

Exercise 3.3

a Read **Section C**, then make your own notes on the story of Thomas Becket.

    i Who are the *two* most important persons in the story?
    ii Which are the *four* most important events in the story?

b Look at **Sources 3f** and **3h**, and read **Source 3g**.

    i Which *two* facts about pilgrims to Canterbury can we learn from **Source 3g**?
    ii Write down *two* facts about pilgrims that we can learn from Sources **3f** and **3h**.

Source 3i

When the Bishop of Winchester died, King Henry III did not look very sad. He set out to make his own half-brother, Aylmer, the new bishop. Aylmer was not even a priest. In any case, he was too young and was not well educated.

    The monks at Winchester have the right to choose the bishop. So the king sent two men there to get them to pick Aylmer. When they failed, the king went to Winchester himself, and made the monks give in.

Written by a monk called Matthew Paris in 1250.

Exercise 3.4

Read **Source 3i**, then read again the notes on **Fact and opinion** on page 14. Write paragraphs for **b** and **c**.

a Write down any *four* **facts** in **Source 3i**.
b What was the author's **opinion** of Aylmer? Did he think that he was the right kind of man to be Bishop of Winchester?
c What do you think was Matthew Paris's **opinion** of the way the new Bishop of Winchester was chosen?

Source 3j

Priests who break the law are tried first by the church courts. The king said that if they are found guilty, they should be sent to the king's court to be punished. Thomas discussed this with the other bishops and abbots. Then he said that what the king wanted was against God's law. The king got angry and told Thomas and the bishops that they had to obey him.

Written by a priest called Henry of Bosham soon after 1170.

Source 3h

Pilgrims leaving Canterbury on their way home.

Causes and reasons

A **cause** is a **reason** for something. It is the answer to the questions '**Why** did it happen?' or '**Why** was it like that?' For example:

    Why did Duke William invade England in 1066?

Often, there is more than one answer to the question **Why**?

    There are a number of **causes** or **reasons** for most things.

Exercise 3.5

Read **Source 3j**. What does **Source 3j** tell us about the **causes** of the quarrel between Henry II and Thomas Becket? Answer questions **a** to **c** in sentences, and question **d** in a paragraph. Use your own words.

a What did King Henry II want to happen to priests who broke the law?
b Why did Thomas disagree?
c Did anyone else agree with Thomas?
d Henry and Thomas had been friends. Do you think this made the king more angry or less? Was it a **cause** of their quarrel?

4 Monks and Friars

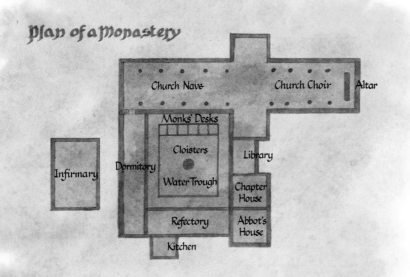

Plan of a Monastery

- Church Nave
- Church Choir
- Altar
- Monks' Desks
- Cloisters
- Library
- Infirmary
- Dormitory
- Water Trough
- Chapter House
- Refectory
- Abbot's House
- Kitchen

A The life of a monk

Monks were men who gave their lives to God. They spent their time praying and working for their fellow men and women. They lived in **monasteries**, under very strict rules. All monks promised to obey their abbot or prior (the head monk). They had to promise not to marry. And they had to give away all their money and goods. The rules laid down every detail of the monks' lives.

MONKS' DAILY TIMETABLE IN SUMMER (IN WINTER SOME OF THE TIMES WERE DIFFERENT)

Out of bed for the first service at midnight.

Back to bed in the dormitory. Straw mattresses were changed once a year.

Second service at 6 a.m.

Washing in cold water in the cloisters.

Breakfast of bread and ale in the refectory. All meals in silence.

Period of work.

Third service - Chapter Mass at 9 a.m.

Chapter – daily meeting at 10 a.m. in chapter house - to discuss business.

High Mass at 11 a.m.

Dinner - no meat allowed.

Private reading.

Nones (fifth service) at 2 p.m.

Work (e.g. copying books). Monks worked in the cloisters.

Vespers (sixth service) at 4 p.m.

More work.

Supper - bread and ale at 6 p.m.

Last service at 7 p.m.

Bed at 7.30 p.m.

For a large part of each day, the monks were in the **choir**. This was the part of the monastery church where they sang and prayed during the services. The local people were sometimes allowed to stand in the **nave**. (Look at the plan of a monastery.)

Monks also had to work. Some cooked and cleaned. Some worked in the fields. Many studied and taught. Others carefully copied out books by hand (the only way of making new books). But they all had to stop when the bell rang for prayer.

Girls might become **nuns**, but only if their fathers were rich. Convents got gifts from the families of new nuns. Like monks, nuns had to make promises, obey rules, and work. Many of them ran schools for girls.

Now try Exercise 4.1.

B Monks and local life

In most places, the monastery's great stone church was the largest building for miles around. The monks played a big part in local life. They looked after the old and sick. They took in travellers who needed a bed for the night.

Monks not only copied books. They also wrote them. Some of them wrote **chronicles**, which were records of things that happened each year. Monks heard the news from travellers who stayed with them. Chronicles written by monks are useful **sources** for students of history.

People who were accused of crimes could ask for **sanctuary** at a monastery. This meant that they could ask to stay there for 40 days. While they were there, no-one could arrest them. To avoid arrest after the 40 days was up, they had to go straight to the nearest

Exercise 4.1

Read **Section A**. Study the cartoons and the monastery plan. Draw your own plan of a monastery, and write in the names of the buildings. Mark the letters **A**, **B**, **C**, **D**, **E**, **F**, and **G** on your plan to show the following:

A The place where the monks slept.
B The part of the church where the monks prayed.
C The place where the monks washed.
D The place where the monks ate their meals.
E The place where the monks held their daily meetings.
F The place where the monks sat when they were copying books.
G The place where sick people were looked after.

Put a key on your plan to show what the letters stand for.

Source 4a

Monks had the tops of their head shaved. This was called the 'tonsure'.

Source **4b**

Source 4c

Durham Cathedral was also a monastery. Anyone wanting sanctuary had to use this knocker on the door.

This picture of a monk comes from a twelfth century book.

port and take the first ship to a foreign country.

Monasteries owned a lot of land. The local peasants worked in their fields. Food from the monasteries' farms fed the monks and their guests. But the monks also sold the spare corn and wool. The money they made paid for the schools and hospitals they ran. What was left paid for extra buildings and decorations for the church.

Now try Exercise 4.2.

Exercise 4.2

Read **Section B**, and study **Sources 4a, 4b, 4c,** and **4d**.
Write your own notes on the following topics. You must use your own words.

a The tonsure
b Sanctuary
c Monks and books
d Monastery farms

Source **4d**

Prior's Hall Barn, Widdington, Essex. It was built about 1400. The prior was the prior of St Valéry in Normandy.

C Friars and Lollards

As time went by, some monks forgot their rules. They allowed themselves better food, including meat. They stopped working in the fields. They began to keep servants to cook and clean for them.

Soon after the year 1200, **St Francis** in Italy and **St Dominic** in Spain started groups of **friars**. The friars had

to be really poor – they had to live as beggars. It was their job to preach the Christian message to the people. By about 1220, there were friars in England.

Monasteries were often in country places, but friars worked in towns. They wore threadbare clothes, went without shoes, and lived in simple shacks. Their only food was what kind people gave them.

The friars were soon very popular Crowds came to hear them preach. Rich men and women gave them money, which the friars kept for themselves. Before long, they too had fine churches, wore warmer clothes, and were looked after by servants.

Men and women complained about rich and lazy bishops, monks, and friars. A teacher at Oxford called **John Wycliffe** said it was time for reform – putting things right. His followers, who were called **Lollards**, drew big crowds when they preached. The bishops began to worry, and got the kings to take their side. Many Lollards were locked up, and some were put to death.

Now try Exercise 4.3.

Exercise 4.3

Read **Section C**, and read **Sources 4e**, **4f**, and **4g**. Now use the sources to find out whether the sentences below are true or false. Write "True" or "False" after each sentence.

Source 4e

a In 1380, the friars still cared only about the poor. _____

d By 1380, the friars had churches of their own. _____

Source 4f

c Some of those who spoke against the church were priests themselves. _____

d People had to pay taxes to the church. _____

e Those who spoke out against the church were popular with ordinary men and women. _____

f You can find nothing written against the church in books written by monks. _____

Source 4g

g At the end of the fourteenth century, monks were still supposed to study and work with their hands. _____

h We do not know whether Chaucer's monk was a rich man. _____

Source 4e

The friars go after the rich folk. They have no time for the poor. No-one can be buried in one of their graveyards or churches unless he leaves them some money in his will.

From *Piers Ploughman*, written by William Langland in about 1380.

Source 4f

William Swinderby was a priest in Leicester. He said that people should not pay tithes to wicked, lazy, or ignorant priests. The bishop was angry, and banned him from preaching in churches. So he set up a pulpit in the street. Crowds from all over flocked to hear him.

Written by Henry Knighton, a monk in Leicester, in 1390. Tithes were taxes which people had to pay to the church.

Source 4g

The monk was keen on hunting. His stable was full of good horses. He found the monastery rules too strict, and let things slide. He said, 'Why should I study in the cloister or work with my hands?'. Riding and hunting the hare were more in his line.

From Geoffrey Chaucer's *Canterbury Tales*, written in about 1390.

A friar preaching.

A monk drinking in secret.

The Scots soldiers had no respect for God or man. They caused ruin to the whole district. Men and women, lords and peasants, were put to death. Towns, churches, and houses were set on fire. The Scots spared no-one, not even the children.

Our abbey stood right in the path of these madmen. So the local people rushed there for refuge. It is a very holy place, with more than one saint buried there. Not even the savage Scots dared to touch it.

Written by a monk called Richard, who lived at Hexham Abbey in 1138, at the time of the Scots invasion.

Primary and secondary sources

Letters and chronicles written by people who were present, and saw the things they wrote about, are called **primary sources**.

Papers and books written by people who were **not present** are called **secondary sources**. The authors of **secondary sources** must have heard about the events from someone else, or read about them in books.

Points of view

Not every word in the sources is true. A lot of authors had their own **point of view**. If they took part in the events, they might belong to one side or the other. Often, they had opinions, or feelings, about what had happened. Some writers might be pleased, or proud. Others could be sad, or afraid. Their points of view sometimes made them **exaggerate** (say things were better or worse than they really were).

Exercise 4.4

Read **Source 4h**. Answer the questions in sentences.

a What is a primary source?
b Who wrote **Source 4h**?
c When did the Scots invasion described in **Source 4h** happen?
d Where was the author of **Source 4h** at the time of the invasion?
e Which words tell us that the Scots did not damage Richard's abbey?
f Is **Source 4h** a primary source? (Give a reason for your answer.)

Exercise 4.5

Read **Source 4h** again. Write a paragraph giving *your* opinions about the following questions.

What do you think was Richard's point of view?
What were Richard's opinions or feelings about the events?
Which parts of **Source 4h** do you think may be exaggerations?
Why do you think Richard may have exaggerated?

Exercise 4.6

Look again at the cartoons on page 20.
Tell the story of a monk's day. (You do not have to include every scene.)

Either (a) write an essay, **or** (b) make a tape

5 The Crusades

A knight 'taking the cross'. He kneels before a priest and promises to serve God. He is wearing the sign of the cross on his surcoat over his chain-mail armour.

A The Kingdom of Jerusalem

Jesus was put to death in **Jerusalem** in Palestine. (Palestine was called **The Holy Land**). So Jerusalem was a holy place for pilgrims. The long journey there was full of danger – from bandits, disease, and shipwreck. But in 1071 the **Turks**, who were Moslems, conquered the Holy Land, and shut the Christian pilgrims out. The pilgrim route was closed.

The Pope was shocked. He urged Christian knights to go and fight a **Crusade** (or holy war) to win back Jerusalem from the Turks. He said that all who took part were sure to go to Heaven.

The Route to the Holy Land

ENGLAND
GERMANY
Atlantic Ocean
FRANCE
Durnstein
AUSTRIA
SPAIN
ITALY
Constantinople
Black Sea
ASIA MINOR
SICILY
CYPRUS
Antioch
THE HOLY LAND
Mediterranean Sea
Acre
Damietta
Jerusalem
EGYPT

→ Richard I's route to the Holy Land
→ Richard I's journey home

On his journey home, Richard I was held prisoner by Duke Leopold at Durnstein.

Christian Kingdoms in the Holy Land

ASIA MINOR
Little Armenia
Edessa
Antioch
ANTIOCH
CYPRUS
Crac des Chevaliers
Tripoli
Beirut
Areas ruled by Moslems in the 12th century
Acre
SYRIA
Kingdom of Jerusalem
Jerusalem
Christian states in the 12th century
EGYPT

Crac des Chevaliers, the great fortress of the Knights Hospitaller (see map on page 25). The Knights Hospitaller were like monks in armour. They were knights who gave their lives to God, and promised to obey their Grand Master. 'Hospitallers' came from all over Europe to the Holy Land.

Hundreds of knights '**took the cross**'. (Look at Source 5a). They made a big sacrifice. They had to leave their wives and families for at least two years. Many of them borrowed money to buy arms and horses, and to pay the wages of the foot-soldiers who came with them.

The knights met at **Constantinople**, then set out in 1097 across Asia Minor. (Look at the maps.) The roads were bad and the food was poor. Most of the men were ill, and many died. But the Crusaders reached **Antioch**, and took it after a siege. Then they headed for Jerusalem.

The Turks fought hard to keep Jerusalem. (It is a holy city for Moslems too.) But in July 1099 the Crusaders broke in. They killed the Turks and destroyed the **mosques** (Moslem temples). Then some Crusaders went home. But others stayed in the Holy Land. They built churches and castles, and chose one of their leaders to be **King of Jerusalem**.

Now try Exercise 5.1.

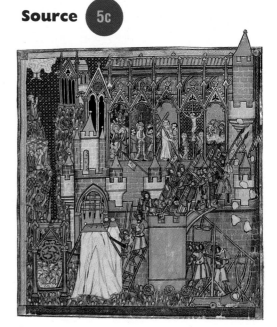

Exercise 5.1

Read **Section A**, then write sentences to show that you know what the following words and phrases mean:

a Pilgrims (Look back to page 18 if you are not sure.)
b The Holy Land
c Crusade
d Taking the cross
e Sacrifice
f Mosque

Source 5b

Crusaders attack a Moslem city. The crusaders are using a catapult to try to break down the city walls.

Source 5c

Crusaders using a siege-tower to attack Jerusalem in 1099.

B Richard the Lion Heart

In 1187, Turks led by **Saladin** took Jerusalem and Acre from the Christians. This made the pope call for a new Crusade. **King Richard I** of England took the cross. (He was so brave that men called him **the Lion Heart**.)

Richard reached the Holy Land in 1191. He, King Philip of France, and Duke Leopold of Austria joined the army trying to take **Acre**. Their **catapults** (see Sources 5b and 5d) threw huge stones at the city walls. The miners dug tunnels underneath. Soldiers fought from **siege-towers** (see Source 5c). Both kings, and most of their men, were ill with fever.

At last, the Turks in Acre gave in. Richard and Philip put their flags on the city walls. But when Leopold did the same, Richard threw the Austrian flag into the moat. Leopold was deeply hurt, and left for home. A short while later, Philip of France set sail too.

Richard stayed, and nearly reached Jerusalem. But he had too few men to take it, and had to turn back. He and Saladin made peace. The Turks kept Jerusalem, but Christian pilgrims could visit it.

Richard set out for England. On his way, he was seized in Austria by Duke Leopold. He was held captive for more than a year. The English had to pay a **ransom** of £100,000 to buy freedom for their king.

Now try Exercises 5.2 and 5.3.

Source 5d

When the crusaders attacked the city of Nicaea in Asia Minor, they used the heads of captured Turks, instead of stones, in their catapults.

Exercise 5.2

Look at **Sources 5b, 5c,** and **5d.** Answer questions **a** to **d** in sentences.

a Which different weapons can you see being used in **Source 5b**?
b What did a catapult do? (Look at **Source 5b.**)
c How do you think Crusaders used siege towers? (Look at **Source 5c.**)
d What are the Crusaders doing in **Source 5d**? Can you think why they are doing this?
e Draw a picture of either a catapult or a siege tower.

Causes and results

Causes come **before** events. Causes are the reasons why the events happen. The conquest of Jerusalem by the Turks was a cause of the Crusades.

Results come **after** events. One result of the first Crusade was that Baldwin of Flanders became King of Jerusalem.

Exercise 5.3

Read **Source 5e**. Then read the following sentences. Some are true and some are false. Write "True" or "False" after each sentence.

a King Philip went home to France. _____ The result was that the duke of Burgundy was put in charge of the French knights in Acre. _____

b There was a war between two sultans. _____ **Source 5e** tells us the cause of the war. _____ One result of the war was that there were not many Turks left in Jerusalem. _____

c The duke of Burgundy turned back. _____ The cause was that he was ill with fever. _____ The result was that the Crusaders did not reach Jerusalem. _____

d Richard threw his tunic over his head. _____ The result was that he did not reach Jerusalem. _____

© Oxford University Press

Source 5e

King Philip of France went home in 1191. But he let his knights remain at Acre. Their leader was the duke of Burgundy. King Richard of England was in charge of the rest of the Crusaders.

Richard and the duke heard that there was war between two sultans, and that very few Turks would be left in Jerusalem. So they set off at once. But they had not gone far when the duke said he was turning back. His reason was that he did not want Richard to get the credit for taking Jerusalem. Richard now had too few knights. When one of them said that he could see Jerusalem ahead, Richard threw his tunic over his head. If he could not capture it, he did not want to see it.

From the *Life of St. Louis*, written by Jean de Joinville in about 1290. Jean de Joinville was born in 1225.

C The failure of the Crusades

Popes kept on urging kings, lords, and knights to go on Crusades. Many answered the call. In English churches you can still see carvings of knights who took the cross.

Why did they go? Some just liked fighting. Some wanted a chance to win fame and glory. But faith in God was the most important thing. Men who had done wrong hoped that their sins would be forgiven. They all believed that Crusaders went to Heaven.

Not only soldiers went on Crusades. Monks, priests, and nuns joined them.

Some kings and lords took their wives. There was even a 'Peasants' Crusade' and a 'Children's Crusade'. Most of the peasants were killed, and a lot of the children were sold as slaves by the Turks.

In the end, the Crusaders failed. They were too few in number, and they were fighting far from home. Too often, they quarrelled among themselves. After 1250, the Turks grew stronger. When Acre fell in 1291, the 'Kingdom of Jerusalem' was at an end.

Now attempt Exercise 5.4.

Motives

Students of history often try to work out the **motives** of the people in the past. **Motives** mean their **reasons** for acting as they did. William the Conqueror's **motive** for invading England was that he wanted to be king.

Turkish mounted archers practising. The Turks wore less armour than the crusaders, so their armies could move quickly.

Source 5f

King Louis jumped into the sea, where the water came up to his armpits. He waded to the shore with his shield hung round his neck. When he reached land, he looked at the enemy and asked who they were. He was told they were Turks. At that, he put his lance under his arm and got ready to charge them. But the Turks fled. We all got onto our horses, and rode with the king to Damietta.

From the *Life of St. Louis*, by Jean de Joinville. This piece describes how St. Louis [King Louis IX of France] arrived in Egypt in 1248.

Exercise 5.4

Read **Section C**, and the notes on **Motives**.
What were the **motives** of the Crusaders?
Read the sentences below. Write out the ones which you think describe the motives of **some** Crusaders.

a Some knights just liked war.
b Crusaders knew that it would be easy to beat the Turks in battle.
c Some knights wanted to win fame for themselves.
d Each Crusader got a sum of money from the king.
e Everyone thought that Crusaders went straight to Heaven when they died.
f The peasants and children probably thought that God would protect them.
g A Crusade was just like a holiday.
h Some queens and ladies went to keep their husbands company.
i Crusaders wanted a change from the boring life at home.

Exercise 5.5

Read **Sources 5e** and **5f**, then answer the questions in sentences.

a Who wrote **Source 5e**, and when was he born?
b When did the events described in **Source 5e** happen?
c Could the author of **Source 5e** have been present when King Richard tried to take Jerusalem?
d Is **Source 5e** a primary or a secondary source?
e Who was the author of **Source 5f**?
f When did the events described in **Source 5f** happen?
g What makes you think that the author of **Source 5f** was present when King Louis landed in Egypt?
h Is **Source 5f** a primary or a secondary source?

Exercise 5.6

Read **Source 5e** again.

Either
a Draw a set of cartoons to tell the story
or
b Say what you think was the duke of Burgundy's opinion of Richard, and Richard's opinion of the duke of Burgundy. (Write two paragraphs.)

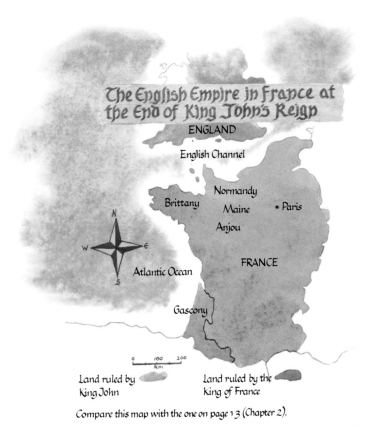

The English Empire in France at the End of King John's Reign

ENGLAND

English Channel

Normandy

Brittany

Maine

• Paris

Anjou

N
W E
S

Atlantic Ocean

FRANCE

Gascony

0   100   200
Km

Land ruled by
King John

Land ruled by the
king of France

Compare this map with the one on page 13 (Chapter 2).

A Magna Carta

After Richard I returned to England, he was soon at war again. This time it was in France. King Philip of France was trying to take back the land in France which belonged to the king of England.

Richard died in 1199, and his brother John became king. But the war in France went on. By 1204, Philip had conquered all of Normandy. (Look at the map.) King John was not the only loser. Many barons had owned land in France as well as England. When Philip drove John out, they lost their French land too.

John kept trying to win Normandy back. He ordered his barons to serve in

King John driven out of France by king Philip

King John and his Barons

King John needed money to pay for an army to win back his lands in France

English barons who owned land in France had to give it up

High taxes (barons paid most)

Barons had to serve in John's army or pay money

Barons who annoyed John were put in prison or made to pay heavy fines

Angry barons

Barons thought that John had murdered his nephew Arthur

his army, or send him money instead. He made the people pay heavy taxes. Men found guilty of crimes were given big fines in court. John spent the money he raised on hiring soldiers to fight in France.

In the end, some of the barons rebelled. John gave in and met their leaders in June 1215 at Runnymede, a meadow near Windsor. The king agreed to put his seal to **Magna Carta** (Latin for 'the great charter').

Magna Carta said that all **free** men had rights. The law of England would protect them. And the king had to obey the law. He could not take free men's money or put free men in prison just as he liked. (This was all right for **free** men, but most people were peasants, and not free.)

Now try Exercise 6.1.

B The beginning of parliament

King John promised to speak to his 'council' before he charged taxes. This council was a meeting of the bishops, abbots, earls, and barons. Soon after King John's time, it began to be called **parliament**. The name comes from the French word 'parler', to speak or talk. So a parliament was where the king talked to the great lords.

John's son, Henry III, also quarrelled with his barons. He too put up taxes without asking their advice. **Simon de Montfort**, who led the rebel barons, was on top for a while, but in the end he lost and was killed in battle. But Henry learned a lesson. In future, he asked parliament to agree to new taxes.

Henry III sometimes asked **knights**

Source 6a

1 Before I make the people pay taxes, I will ask the advice of the lords in my council.
2 No free man may be arrested or put in prison unless other free men decide that he is guilty, and unless he has a proper trial.
3 Judges will not be allowed to take bribes.
4 People found guilty in court will not have to pay bigger fines than they can afford.
5 Barons will be fined only if the other barons say they are guilty.

(Some of the promises made by King John in Magna Carta.)

Exercise 6.1

Read **Section A** and **Source 6a**, and look at the cartoon.

a Write down *four* things that made the barons angry with King John.
b Which *two* promises in Magna Carta (**Source 6a**) would most please the barons?
c Which *three* promises in Magna Carta (**Source 6a**) made sure that free men were treated properly by the courts?

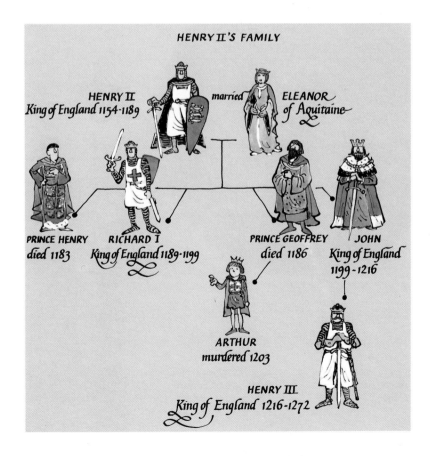

HENRY II'S FAMILY

HENRY II
King of England 1154-1189   married   ELEANOR of Aquitaine

PRINCE HENRY
died 1183

RICHARD I
King of England 1189-1199

PRINCE GEOFFREY
died 1186

JOHN
King of England 1199-1216

ARTHUR
murdered 1203

HENRY III
King of England 1216-1272

of the shire to come to his parliaments. These knights owned land, but were not as rich as the barons. Later, the **boroughs**, or main towns, were told to send **burgesses**. Burgess just means townsman, but the burgesses who came to parliament were always rich merchants. These knights and burgesses were the first 'common' men, or **commons**, to sit in parliament.

By the end of the thirteenth century, parliament met quite often. It contained both great lords and commons. It had the right to say 'Yes' or 'No' to taxes. And it had the power to make **statutes**, or new laws.

Now try Exercise 6.2.

Above: King John's seal, which he fixed to Magna Carta to show that he had agreed to accept it.

Right: King Edward I with his parliament. King Alexander III of Scotland is on Edward's right, and Llyewelyn II, Prince of Wales, is on his left.

Exercise 6.2

Read **Section B**, then fill in the blank spaces in the following sentences. Use words or dates from the list below. (You will not need all of them.)

treaties   knights   taxes   1400   burgesses   bishops

kings   law   villages   1300   statutes   lords   peasants

1200   towns

a Parliament at first was a meeting between the king and his great _____ .

b _____ of the shire were landowners who were not as rich as the barons.

c Boroughs were the main _____ .

d _____ were the men who were sent by the towns to parliament.

e The commons were the _____ of the shire and the _____ .

f By the end of the thirteenth century, parliament had the power to charge _____ and make _____ .

g A statute was a new _____ .

C Lords and commons

England's kings were always short of money to pay for their wars. So they often had to ask parliament for new taxes. They found that they could not manage without parliament's help.

The most important men in parliament were still the lords. Wise kings listened to their advice. Two kings, Edward II and Richard II, were **deposed** (thrown out) in the fourteenth century because they would not listen to the lords. By 1450, when Henry VI was king, the great lords were stronger than the king.

At the same time, the commons had won some rights. After 1327, they *always* took part in parliaments. By the fifteenth century, new taxes and statutes *had* to be passed by the commons as well as the lords. But there was still no 'House of Commons' or 'House of Lords'. Parliament did not always meet in London, and there were no 'Houses of Parliament'.

Now try Exercise 6.3.

How useful are the sources?

We should not always believe the sources. It is a good idea to ask questions about them, for example:

- Who wrote this source and when?
- Was this person there when the event happened?
- Did this person have a reason to be biased (tell a one-sided story)?
- Could this person have got hold of false information?

The Abbey of Bury St. Edmunds in Suffolk – the lords and commons were told to join King Edward I here in 1296. Parliament did not always meet in London.

Exercise 6.3

Read **Section C**, and read **Section A** again.
How did things change between the time of King John (early thirteenth century) and the time of King Henry VI (mid-fifteenth century)?

Fill in the spaces in the chart. Under **John** and **Henry VI**, write **Yes** or **No**. Under **Change**, write **Change** or **No Change**.

	John	Henry VI	Change?
Was the king often at war?		Yes	
Did the king need money?		Yes	
Did they use the word "parliament"?	No		
Were the lords important?			
Did the commons take part in parliament?			
Were there any "Houses of Parliament"?			

© Oxford University Press

Source 6b

The devil has stirred up the barons of England against you. They have dared to make war on you. They have forced you to agree to a charter which is illegal and unfair. I completely condemn this charter. I order you not to keep it.

Letter from the pope to King John in 1216.

Source 6c

In the year 1215, in a place called Runnymede, King John put his great seal on Magna Carta. It was a great event in English history. It meant that from that time on, kings must obey the law. The law gave rights to all men, and kings could not take them away.

Adapted from comments by Professor W. S. McKechnie in 1915.

Source 6d

My next parliament will be held at Easter 1275 in London. All the bishops, abbots, and nobles will be there. I order you to send four knights from your county to the parliament. You must also send four or six good men from each town.

Letter from Edward I [written by one of his clerks] to the sheriff of Middlesex in 1275. Each sheriff would get the same kind of letter.

Source 6e

The nobles gathered at Oxford for the parliament. They ordered their knights to come with them, to defend them from their enemies. They were afraid that the king and his half-brothers from France would attack them. When parliament opened, the nobles told King Henry III that he must keep his promise to obey Magna Carta.

Written by a monk called Matthew Paris at St. Albans Abbey in 1259. Matthew did not go to the Oxford parliament himself.

Exercise 6.4

Not everyone thinks the same about the events of the past. For example, there have been many different opinions about Magna Carta. Read **Sources 6b** and **6c**, then answer the questions in sentences.

a Who wrote **Source 6b**, and when?
b The author of **Source 6b** said that the barons had done two things which were wrong. What were they?
c Did the author of **Source 6b** think that the king could do as he liked?
d Who wrote **Source 6c**, and when?
e **Source 6c** was written how many years after **Source 6b**?
f Did the author of **Source 6c** think that the barons were wicked?
g Why did the author of **Source 6c** think that Magna Carta was important?

Exercise 6.5

Read **Sources 6d** and **6e**. Then answer questions **a** to **g** in sentences and question **h** in a paragraph.

a Who wrote **Source 6d**, and when?
b On whose orders was **Source 6d** written?
c What does **Source 6d** tell us about the parliament of 1275?
d Should we believe what **Source 6d** tells us about the parliament of 1275?
e Who wrote **Source 6e**, and when?
f Was the author of **Source 6e** present at the Oxford parliament?
g How might the author of **Source 6e** have got to know what happened?
h Can you think of any reasons why the author of **Source 6e** might have got things wrong?

The tomb of King John in Worcester Cathedral.

7 Wales in the Middle Ages

A Wales and the marcher earls

Wales is a land of hills and mountains. In the Middle Ages, its people lived mostly by rearing cattle and hunting. They spent much of their time fighting each other, or the English. But they were also fond of music and poetry. And they were proud of their ancient Welsh language.

There was never a king of Wales. Each district had its chief, who fought wars with his neighbours. Sometimes, one man made himself master of a large part of Wales. But when he died, his land was split up among his sons.

William I did not try to conquer the whole of Wales. He gave land on the Welsh border to his most trusted lords.

We call them **marcher earls** or **lords of the marches**. (March means border.) They were allowed to build castles, raise armies, and fight as much as they liked with the Welsh.

The marcher earls conquered part of south Wales. They built castles (such as Cardiff and Pembroke) and brought in English peasants to farm the land. But strong Welsh chiefs, such as the **Lord Rhys**, could get the better of the marcher earls and trouble their king. Henry II made peace with Rhys in 1171, leaving him in charge of most of Wales.

Now try Exercise 7.1.

A Welsh chief's castle at Dolbadarn in north Wales.

Source **7a**

The Welsh are good horsemen. They are quick on their feet, and not fussy about what they eat. They are very different from Norman knights. In Normandy, they fight on flat land, but here all battles are on rough ground. In Normandy, there are open fields, but here there is forest. In Normandy, captured knights are ransomed, but here they are put to death. Norman knights wear heavy iron armour. The Welsh wear light armour, so that they can move easily, and fight on foot if they have to.

From a book about Wales, written by a priest called Gerald in 1188.

Wales in the Middle Ages

ANGLESEY
Beaumaris
Degannwy
Conwy
Rhuddlan
Flint
Chester
Caernarfon
Dolbadarn
GWYNEDD
Harlech
Shrewsbury
Irish Sea
Ludlow
St. Davids
Milford Haven
Pembroke
Caerffili
Chepstow
Cardiff

0   20   40   60
Km

Land more than 500 metres above sea level.

Land between 200 and 500 metres above sea level.

Land less than 200 metres above sea level.

— Border with England

Exercise 7.1

Read **Section A** and **Source 7a**.

a Write down *three* important facts about the country of Wales.
b Write down *three* important facts about Welsh fighting men.
c Write down *three* facts about the marcher earls.

B The Llywelyns and Edward I

The greatest Welsh princes were the two **Llywelyns**, grandfather and grandson. Like Rhys, they were leaders of bands of archers and spearmen who could face and beat the famous Norman knights. But also like Rhys, they were wise judges and fair rulers as well.

In the time of King John, **Llywelyn I** was a prince of **Gwynedd**. (Look at the map.) He conquered his neighbours, and became the ruler of most of Wales. King Henry III of England kept on good terms with him.

When Llywelyn I died in 1240, his kingdom fell apart. His grandson, **Llywelyn II**, had to fight his way back to power. But by 1258 he was strong enough to call himself '**Prince of Wales**'. And when Edward I became king in 1272, Llywelyn II refused to do homage. This was Llywelyn's way of saying, 'Keep out! The king of England has no rights in Wales'.

That meant war. Edward I invaded north Wales. He used his navy to seize Anglesey, where the corn that fed Llywelyn's men grew. The prince made peace, but it did not last. A new revolt began in 1282, but the outcome was bad for Wales. Llywelyn was killed in battle. His brother Dafydd (David) was captured and hanged. The two brothers' heads were stuck on lances and put on show in London.

Edward wanted no more trouble from Wales. He carved it up into counties, like England, with a sheriff in charge of each. He gave Wales English courts, which used English law. Thousands of English workmen were sent to build a string of castles round Gwynedd. (Look at the map.)

Now try Exercise 7.2.

Now try Exercise 7.2.

Exercise 7.2

Read **Section B**, then answer the questions.
Write your answers in sentences.

a What do you think was Henry III's **motive**, or **reason**, for staying friendly with Llywelyn I?
b What do you think was Llywelyn II's **motive** for refusing to do homage to Edward I?
c What do you think was Edward I's **motive** for putting Llywelyn's and Dafydd's heads on show?
d What do you think was Edward I's **motive** for building a ring of castles round Gwynedd?

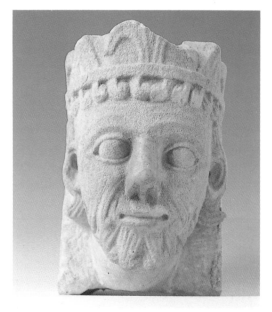

Far left: A thirteenth-century drawing showing Llywelyn I on his deathbed.

Left: A carved stone head from Deganwy, said to show Llywelyn II.

Caerffili Castle in south Wales. It was built by a great marcher earl called Gilbert de Clare.

C Glyn Dŵr and Tudor

In 1301, Edward I made his own son 'Prince of Wales'. He thought that this would bring the English and Welsh together. Since then, 'Prince of Wales' has always been the title of the king or queen of England's eldest son. Not many of them have learned to speak Welsh.

For a few years after the conquest of Wales, the Welsh stopped fighting each other and the English. But they did not all live in peace. English kings were glad to have Welsh archers in their armies. And young Welshmen were keen to earn money by fighting for the English against the Scots and French (see Chapter 10).

Some Welshmen still dreamed of a free Wales. **Owain Glyn Dŵr** (Owen Glendower) was the son of a Welsh chief. He studied law in London, and served in the English army. But when some English earls rebelled against King Henry IV in 1400, Owain joined in. He raised an army of Welshmen

A Welsh archer

and captured the king's Welsh castles. His men made him Prince of Wales.

All went well for a time. Then Henry hit back. He beat the English earls, invaded Wales, and won back his castles. Owain was killed in battle. Henry passed harsh laws which said that Welshmen could not carry arms or hold meetings. Wales was as good as part of England.

In a way, though, the Welsh were the winners in the end. **Henry Tudor**, who was a quarter Welsh, grabbed the throne of England in 1485 (see Chapter 12). Henry came by ship from France to Milford Haven in Wales. As he marched through Wales, a lot of Welshmen joined his army. They carried with them the red dragon flag of Wales. When Henry became king of England, he kept Welsh poets and singers at his court.

Now try Exercises 7.3 and 7.4.

Exercise 7.3

Read **Sections A, B and C**.
We call the years 1101 to 1130 the **early twelfth century**.
The years 1131 to 1170 are the **mid-twelfth century**.
The years from 1171 to 1200 are the **late twelfth century**.
Complete the sentences below.

a William the Conqueror invaded south Wales in 1081 (in the _____ eleventh century.)

b Owain Gwynedd ruled most of north Wales between 1137 and 1170 (in the _____ twelfth century.)

c Llywelyn I died in 1240 (in the mid-_____ century).

d Llywelyn II called himself 'Prince of Wales' in 1258 (in the _____ _____ century).

e Edward I made his son 'Prince of Wales' in 1301 (in the _____ _____ century).

f Henry Tudor landed at Milford Haven in 1485 (in the _____ _____ century).

Exercise 7.4

Historians have different **opinions** about the past.
You have to use the **facts** to decide which opinions you agree with and which ones you are against. You often find some facts on one side, and some on the other.
Think about this opinion:
  'After 1301, the Welsh were quite happy to be ruled by the English. And the English expected no trouble from the Welsh.'

a Write down any facts in Section C which might make you **agree with** the opinion.

b Write down any facts which might make you **disagree with** the opinion.

Source 7b

Last Sunday I came to the town of Flint, with its great double walls and huge gates. I would like to see it on fire! There was a wedding feast going on there. But there wasn't much to drink – it was an English feast.

I tried to earn a few pence by singing some songs and playing my harp. But the guests just mocked me and jeered at me. Those simple farmers know nothing about music. They chattered about peas and manure as I sang. They sent me away with nothing, not even a bowl of bean soup. I won't go near Flint or its English people again.

From a fifteenth-century Welsh poem.

Exercise 7.5

Read **Source 7b**, then answer the questions in sentences.

a Write down as many **facts** as you can find about the *town* of Flint.
b Write down as many **facts** as you can find about the *people* of Flint.
c What was the wedding guests' **opinion** of Welsh music?
d What was the author's **opinion** of the wedding guests?
e What was the author's **opinion** of Flint?

Source 7c

Harlech Castle from the south. The houses on the hillside were not there when Edward I built the castle to keep the Welsh under control.

Source 7d

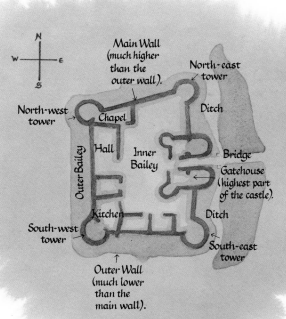

Exercise 7.6

Look at **Sources 7c** and **7d**.

a Draw a copy of the plan of Harlech Castle (**Source 7d**).
b Compare **Sources 7c** and **7d**.
  i Which parts of the castle can you see in **Source 7c**?
  ii Which parts can you not see?
c Harlech Castle was strong and difficult to attack.
  Either
  i Describe in writing how the Welsh might have attacked it. Say which would be the hardest parts of the castle to capture.
  Or
  ii Draw a set of cartoons to show an attack on Harlech Castle.

Scotland in the Middle Ages

A The King of England's vassal?

The peasants of Scotland were poor. They kept cattle, and grew some oats and barley. They lived in wood and earth shacks, which they shared with the animals. At first, most people spoke **Gaelic**, but English slowly spread from the south and east.

In the Middle Ages, Scotland had its own king. He was often at war. He fought the king of **Norway**, who owned the islands of the west and north. He fought the king of England, his neighbour to the south. And he fought his own chiefs and lords. (Each chief had a band of fierce peasant soldiers.)

There was no Norman Conquest of Scotland. But **David I**, who was king from 1124 to 1153, invited some Norman knights to settle in Scotland. The knights did **homage** to the king, and became his **vassals**, or servants. With Norman knights in his army, David was a much stronger king.

These chess pieces, carved from walrus ivory, were found on the Isle of Lewis in the Hebrides. They were made in the early thirteenth century. At that time, the Hebrides belonged to Norway.

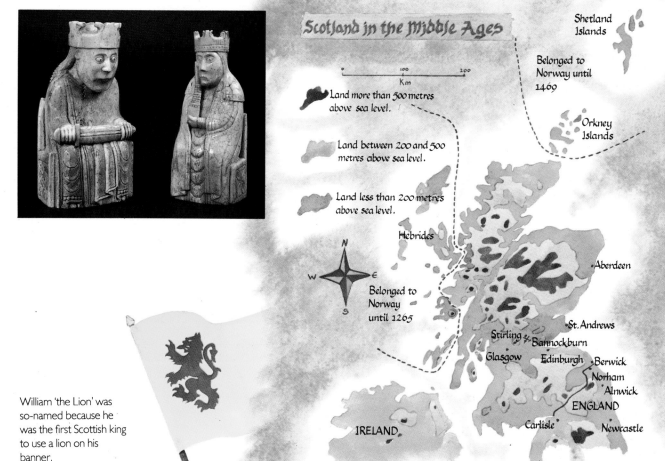

Scotland in the Middle Ages

Km

Land more than 500 metres above sea level.

Land between 200 and 500 metres above sea level.

Land less than 200 metres above sea level.

Shetland Islands

Belonged to Norway until 1469

Orkney Islands

Hebrides

Belonged to Norway until 1265

Aberdeen

St. Andrews

Stirling

Bannockburn

Glasgow

Edinburgh

Berwick

Norham

Alnwick

ENGLAND

IRELAND

Carlisle

Newcastle

William 'the Lion' was so-named because he was the first Scottish king to use a lion on his banner.

King **William the Lion**, David's grandson, led his knights against the Highland chiefs and forced them to obey him. But in a war with England in 1174, he was captured. Henry II of England did not set him free until William did homage and became **his** vassal.

Now try Exercise 8.1

Dates

Dates are useful things. They tell us which order events happened in. They tell us how old people were at certain points in their lives. They tell us how much time passed between events.

For example, King David I of Scotland was born in 1084, and became king in 1124. If we take away 1084 from 1124, we get the answer 40. So David I was 40 years old when he became king.

B **The War of Independence**

For a time there was peace, but trouble began again in 1286 when King Alexander III died. The next in line to the throne was a girl of three, Margaret, the **Maid of Norway**. (Look at the family tree.) And in 1290 Margaret herself died on her way from Norway to Scotland.

Thirteen men now claimed the right to be king. The Scots asked **Edward I** of England to choose a king for them. Edward picked **John Balliol**, and John did **homage** to Edward. This made Edward think that he could treat the king of Scotland as one of his **vassals**. When John Balliol and the Scots objected, there was war. The Scots were beaten, John gave up the throne, and Edward took control of Scotland.

Exercise 8.1

Read Section A, and read the notes on **Dates**.
Look at the list of dates, which are all to do with Scottish history.

1141 Malcolm IV was born.
1143 William the Lion was born.
1153 Malcolm IV became king.
1165 Malcolm IV died and William the Lion became king.
1174 William the Lion was captured at Alnwick in Northumberland.
1214 William the Lion died.

Now answer the questions.

a Malcolm IV and William the Lion were brothers. Which of them was the elder? _____

b How old was Malcolm IV when he became king? _____

c For how long was Malcolm IV king of Scotland? _____

d How old was William the Lion when he became king? _____

e How old was William the Lion when he was captured? _____

f For how long was William the Lion king? _____

g How old was William the Lion when he died? _____

© Oxford University Press

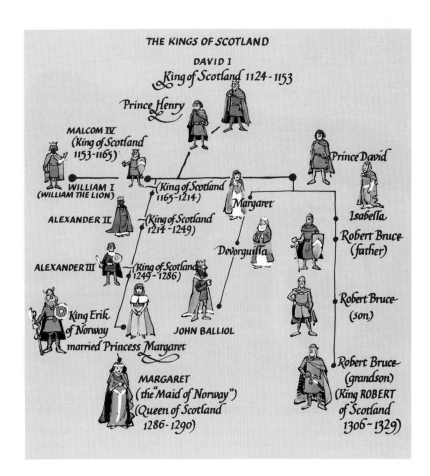

THE KINGS OF SCOTLAND

Some Scots, led by **William Wallace**, rebelled. They beat an English army in 1297. Scots **national feeling** was on their side. But when Edward came north again they fled to the hills and forests. At last, in 1305 Wallace was captured. He was taken to London, tried, and put to death as a **traitor**.

The Scots took heart when Edward himself died in 1307. His son, **Edward** II, was a poor leader. And the Scots now had **Robert Bruce** as their general and king. Bruce's army won battles and took castles from the English in a war that lasted from 1307 to 1314. It ended in a great Scots victory at **Bannockburn**, near Stirling, in June 1314. The English left Scotland – the Scots had won their **War of Independence**.

Now try Exercise 8.2.

The two sides of King Alexander II's seal show him as a judge and a soldier.

The Scots did not have as many guns as the English. 'Mons Meg' was one of their few cannon. It was made in Flanders in about 1450. You can still see it in Edinburgh Castle.

Exercise 8.2

Read **Section B**, and look at the family tree.

a Who do you think are the *three* most important people in the story? Write a sentence about each, saying why he or she is important.)
b What do you think are the *four* most important events in the story?

C The 'Auld Alliance'

After Bannockburn, England and Scotland were often at war. They quarrelled about land – the town of Berwick changed hands thirteen times. Both sides complained about thieves who crossed the border to steal their cattle.

For all this time, Scotland's kings kept on good terms with France, England's other enemy. The French kings were pleased if the English had to fight the Scots – it meant they had fewer troops to send to France. The Scots called this friendship the '**Auld Alliance**'.

After Robert Bruce, though, the Scots did badly in their wars. England had more men, and it was a richer country. So its king could afford bigger armies and more modern weapons. Also, the Scots lords were always fighting with each other, and with their king. They made Scotland much weaker than it should have been.

Things improved in the time of **James IV**, who became king in 1488. James was a bright young man, keen on all kinds of art and science. He made the Scots lords obey the law, and gave his country peace for a while. But then the French talked him into invading England. He and most of his lords were killed at the battle of **Flodden** in 1513.

Now try Exercise 8.3.

Exercise 8.3

Read **Section C**.

a What were the **causes** of the wars between England and Scotland?
b **Why** was the king of France glad to have Scotland as an ally?
c Write down three **reasons** why the Scots did badly in the wars.

An extract from the Aberdeen Breviary – one of the first books printed in Scotland during the reign of James IV. The first printing press in England was set up by William Caxton in 1477.

Source

You seized my castles and land without any excuse. You robbed me and my subjects. You took Scotsmen off to England to be prisoners in your castles. Things just go from bad to worse. Now you have crossed the border with a great army and have started killing and burning.

Part of a letter from John Balliol to Edward I, written in 1296.

Source

John Balliol, the king of Scotland, promised to obey me. Then he and some of his nobles began to plot against me. English ships that were in Scottish ports were burned, and the sailors were killed. An army of Scots invaded England. They burned villages, monasteries, and churches. In one place, they set fire to a school with the children still in it. I could stand it no more. So I declared war and invaded Scotland.

Part of a letter from Edward I to the Pope, written in 1301.

Exercise 8.4

Read **Sources 8a** and **8b**. They are both about the beginning of war between England and Scotland in 1296. Answer questions **a** to **e** in sentences.

a **Source 8a** says that the war was whose fault?
b What complaints does John Balliol make? (Use your own words.)
c **Source 8b** says that the war was whose fault?
d What complaints does Edward I make? (Use your own words.)
e Which fact is mentioned in both sources?
f Why do you think the sources are so different? (Write a paragraph.)

Source 8c

Wallace lived by robbery in the forests and hills. King Edward said he would give £200 to any man who killed Wallace. At last, Sir John Menteith captured him. He was taken to London, and tried for treason, theft, and murder. They cut off his head and cut his body into four parts to show people what happens to traitors and thieves.

Written by a monk in Bridlington in Yorkshire in the early fourteenth century.

Source 8d

Wallace led the 'common folk' of Scotland. This was why Edward I hated him so much. Edward knew that if the people were against him he would never rule Scotland in peace. So he called Wallace a traitor. And when he caught him, he had him put to death. Edward hoped that this savage act would make all Scots people fear him, and obey. But the murder of their hero just made the 'common folk' of Scotland hate the English more.

Written by a Scottish historian called E. M. Barrow in 1934. (Adapted.)

Source 8e

King James IV of Scotland. This portrait was painted in the seventeenth century by Daniel Mytens. He probably saw an earlier picture of James IV, painted by an artist who knew the king.

Exercise 8.5

Read **Sources 8c** and **8d**, then discuss these questions in a group.

a Who wrote the sources? When and where did they live?
b What did the two authors think of William Wallace?
c Did the two authors think that Edward I treated Wallace fairly?
d Can you think of any reasons why the two authors had different opinions of Wallace and Edward I?

One person should give a talk to the rest of the class (or make a tape) saying what your answers to the questions are.

Exercise 8.6

Look at **Source 8e**, then answer the questions in sentences.

a **Source 8e** is a portrait of which king of Scotland? When did he live?
b What does **Source 8e** tell us about the appearance of the king?
c **Source 8e** tells us that the king was keen on which sport?
d When was the portrait painted? Could it have been painted from life?
e How did the painter know what the king looked like?
f Should we trust what **Source 8e** tells us about the king? (Write two or three sentences.)

9 Ireland in the Middle Ages

Ireland in the Middle Ages

ULSTER • Carrick-fergus

CONNAUGHT

R.Shannon + Kells

Atlantic Ocean

Clonmacnoise + Durrow + • Dublin
Clonfort + The Pale

LEINSTER Irish Sea

Limerick • Clara

Jerpoint +
Waterford • • Wexford

MUNSTER

N
W E
S

Land more than 500 metres above sea level.

Land between 200 and 500 metres above sea level.

Land less than 200 metres above sea level.

+ Important monasteries

0   100   200 Kms
0   62   124 miles

A Dermot and Strongbow

In the Middle Ages the Irish were mainly cattle-farmers. They used cows, not coins, as money. But they were not backward. They had been Christians for hundreds of years. Irish priests took the Christian message to many parts of Europe. Irish monks ran schools, and they were very fine artists.

The only towns in Ireland had been built by the **Vikings**. These raiders from Norway had come to rob and burn, but had stayed to trade. **Dublin** was their chief base.

Each part of Ireland had its own king, and they spent a lot of time fighting each other. A 'high king of Ireland' was supposed to rule over

When the Vikings raided Ireland, the monks in many monasteries built tall round-towers. These were look-out posts and strong places where the monks could take refuge.

Irish monks were famous all over Europe as scholars and artists. This page from the *Book of Kells* is an example of their work. It was written in about AD 800, long before the Normans came to England.

them all, but most high kings were weak. **Brian Boru** was different. He made the Irish combine to fight the Vikings in 1014. The Irish won, but Brian was killed in the battle.

Rory O'Connor, who was high king in 1166, fell out with **Dermot**, the king of Leinster. Dermot was banished (forced to leave Ireland). He made his way to the court of King Henry II of England, to ask for help.

Henry said that his lords and knights could go with Dermot to Ireland if they wished. One of those who went was **Richard of Clare**, whose nickname was 'Strongbow'. He won back Leinster for Dermot, and married Dermot's daughter. When Dermot died, Strongbow became King of Leinster.

Now try Exercise 9.1.

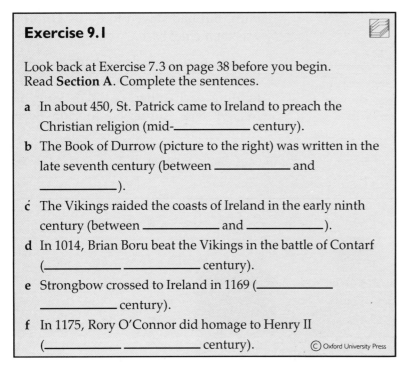

Exercise 9.1

Look back at Exercise 7.3 on page 38 before you begin.
Read **Section A**. Complete the sentences.

a In about 450, St. Patrick came to Ireland to preach the Christian religion (mid-_____ century).

b The Book of Durrow (picture to the right) was written in the late seventh century (between _____ and _____).

c The Vikings raided the coasts of Ireland in the early ninth century (between _____ and _____).

d In 1014, Brian Boru beat the Vikings in the battle of Contarf (_____ _____ century).

e Strongbow crossed to Ireland in 1169 (_____ _____ century).

f In 1175, Rory O'Connor did homage to Henry II (_____ _____ century).

© Oxford University Press

A page from the *Book of Durrow* – it was written before AD 700.

B **Ireland nearly conquered**

Henry II did not want Strongbow to be a king. In 1171 he himself crossed to Ireland with his army. He did not need to do much fighting. Strongbow **did homage** to him. The Irish kings and chiefs did the same. Each of them promised to pay Henry so many cows' hides each year.

Henry left Ireland after six months. But some of his lords and knights stayed to fight and conquer. Soon there were castles (wood and earth at first, stone later) all over the eastern half of Ireland.

Henry gave his youngest son, John, the title **lord of Ireland**, and sent him there on a visit in 1185. The Irish chiefs, in their long robes, came to Dublin to do homage to him. But John and his young friends were foolish.

They laughed at the chiefs and pulled their beards. The Irish went home in disgust.

When John himself was king, he came back to Ireland. He acted more wisely this time, and showed respect to the Irish. He built castles and appointed judges, and brought law and order to at least part of the land.

English rule spread westwards in the thirteenth century. Irish peasants tilled the fields, and English lords lived in the castles. Some towns grew up, but the men and women in them were English, or Welsh, or French. They used money in the towns, but most Irishmen still counted in cows or cows' skins.

Now try Exercise 9.2.

Source 9a

> *From north to south, Ireland stretches a distance of eight days at 40 miles a day. From east to west, it stretches for four days. The country is low-lying round the coast. Inland it rises up to hills and mountains. The Shannon is the biggest river. Its source is in a lake that lies between Connaught and Munster. From there, part of it flows south to Limerick and the sea. The other part flows north between Ulster and Connaught. It reaches the sea in the north.*

From a book written by a Welsh priest called Gerald in about 1190.

Exercise 9.2

Read **Section B** and **Source 9a**, and look at the map of Ireland on page 45. Was Gerald (the author of **Source 9a**) right about Ireland? Fill in the blank spaces.

a Gerald said that Ireland stretches _____ miles from north to south. He said that it stretches _____ miles from east to west.

b The map shows that Ireland is _____ miles long from north to south, and _____ miles wide from east to west.

c Gerald was _____ when he said that there are hills and mountains in Ireland. But he was _____ when he said they were not near the coast.

d In some ways, Gerald was right about the River Shannon:
  i It is Ireland's _____ river.
  ii It does flow south to _____ and the sea.

e In some ways, Gerald was wrong about the Shannon:
  i Its source is not in a _____ between Connaught and Munster.
  ii Part of it does not flow _____ .

C **The Irish strike back**

The Irish did not give in to the English. After the year 1250, they began to get on top. The English had to fall back to the east coast of Ireland. By 1400, they ruled only the **Pale**, the district round Dublin.

One reason for the change was that the Irish got help from Scotland. The Scots soldiers could stand up to and beat the English knights. A second reason was that the English kings had no soldiers to spare for Ireland. They were too busy with wars in Wales, Scotland, and France.

A third reason for the Irish success had nothing to do with war. Most English (and French) lords and knights who stayed in Ireland married Irish girls. Their sons, and *their* sons, also took Irish wives. In time, they became completely Irish.

The great lords were vassals of the English king. But they and their families spoke the Irish language. They kept Irish poets in their homes. They were keen on stories of Irish heroes, giants, and magic. They had no time for English laws and taxes.

Now try Exercise 9.3.

Source **9b**

You are not proper Irishmen. You cut your hair short in the English style. You should leave it long and curling as the Irish do. No Irish hero ever wore English breeches, or jewelled spurs, or a fancy cloak. They didn't wear ruffs round their necks or gold rings on their fingers. They lived in wattle houses, not stone castles.

From a sixteenth-century Irish poem.

Source **9c**

A group of soldiers and peasants in Ireland, drawn in 1521.

Exercise 9.3

Read **Section C**. Then read **Source 9b** and look at **Source 9c**.

a   How were the Irish and English different, according to **Source 9b**? Make your own notes about the following
   i Hair-style
   ii Clothes
   iii Jewellery
   iv Houses
b   Which are the peasants in **Source 9c**? What makes you think they are poor? (Write two or three sentences.)

Source 9d

The monks of Clonmacnoise were having a meeting. Suddenly, they looked up and saw a ship. It was sailing over them in the air, as if it were on the sea. When the crew of the ship saw the monks, they dropped an anchor. A man came out of the ship, swimming as if he were in the water. The monks tried to reach him, but he said, 'Let me go, you are drowning me'.

This story was told by a fourteenth century Irish poet. Another poet told the same story a hundred years earlier.

Two Irish pilgrim monks, St Columbanus and St Gallus, being rowed across Lake Constance, Switzerland, while travelling in Europe.

Exercise 9.5

Read the notes on 'different kinds of evidence'. How would *you* go about discovering more about Ireland in the Middle Ages? What kinds of evidence would be useful? Study the list below.

  i Reading books that were written in the Middle Ages.
  ii Talking to people who lived in the Middle Ages.
  iii Looking at drawings and pictures made in the Middle Ages.
  iv Visiting old houses, castles, and churches.
  v Looking at photographs taken in the Middle Ages.
  vi Looking at carvings in churches or on gravestones.
  vii Visiting museums where they have articles from the Middle Ages.

a Write down all the things in the list which would be useful ways of finding out more about Medieval Ireland.
Write a sentence about each, saying what you might learn from it.
b Which things have you left out? Write a sentence about each, saying why you have left it out.

Exercise 9.4

Read **Source 9d**.
Which of these statements do you think is true?

a The story is pure fiction. Probably no-one ever believed it.
b The story can not be true, but at the time the Irish people probably believed it.
c There are some true things in the story. (Look at the map.) Most of it is fiction, but some people may have believed it.
d The story may be true.

Write out the statement which you think is true. Write a paragraph giving your reasons.

Different kinds of evidence

The **sources** help us in different ways. For example, old books give us the names of people in the past, and tell us what they did. Old pictures show us how they dressed.

A student of history must know **what kind of evidence** he or she is looking for. And he or she must know where to look for it.

Exercise 9.6

In your own words, tell the story of Dermot and Strongbow (see **Sections A** and **B**). Begin with the quarrel between Dermot and Rory O'Connor, and end with the Irish kings doing homage to Henry II.
(Write the story out, or make a tape, or tell the story in pictures.)

Life on the Land

From the air, you can still see signs of the strips in Padbury's open fields.

A Open-field villages

Nine out of ten people in the Middle Ages worked on the land. In Wales, Scotland, Ireland, and the north-west of England, the peasants (country people) kept sheep and cattle, and grew only a few crops. They lived on farms or in small hamlets. But in the Midlands and the east of England, the peasants tilled the land and lived in villages.

In the time of the Normans, a lot of English villages had two large **open fields**. The fields were divided into long, narrow **strips**. Each peasant would have some strips in one field, and some in the other.

Source 10a

Taking the grain to the mill.

Above, stacking the crop.   *Below*, harrowing to cover the seed.

Each year, the peasants grew crops in **one** of the two fields. All of them worked together to plough, sow the seed, and harrow the land to cover the seed with soil. When the wheat or barley or beans had grown, everyone joined in the work of harvest. Each man kept the crops which grew on his strips.

The other open field was left **fallow**. This meant that nothing but grass grew there. Animals were allowed to graze there, and their manure made the soil richer. The next year, the fallow field would be used to grow crops, and the first field would be left fallow.

As well as the open fields, each village had a meadow for hay. And there was some **common** land, where the peasants' sheep and cattle could graze. In the winter there was not enough food for the animals. So the peasants had to kill most of the animals in the autumn. They salted the meat to preserve it. They ate some, and sold the rest.

Now try Exercises 10.1 and 10.2.

Exercise 10.1

Read **Section A**.
Write six sentences to show that you know what each of the words below means. Use your own words if you can.

a peasant
b open fields
c strips
d fallow
e meadow
f common

Exercise 10.2

The pictures in **Source 10A** show peasants in the Middle Ages doing farm work – milling, stacking, harrowing, reaping (or harvesting), ploughing and sowing. Each of these jobs had to be done at the right time of the year.

a Put the six jobs into the right order and write them in a list.
b Copy one of the pictures. Add labels to explain what is happening.

Above, reaping (harvesting) the crop.

Below, ploughing the field.

Sowing the seed.

B The lord of the manor and the peasants

The most important man in the village was the **lord of the manor**. (Manor is another word for village.) The land belonged to the lord, and the peasants had to pay him rent.

Most peasants were **villeins**. Villeins were not free, nor were their wives and children. They could not leave the village unless the lord of the manor said so. They paid rent to the lord by working two or three days a week on his land. Many of them paid money as well, and they had to give him hens at Christmas and eggs at Easter. At harvest time, they did extra work, called 'boon days'. (Where does the modern word 'villain' come from?)

A villein's corn was milled in the lord's mill, and the lord got a share of the flour. If a villein's daughter got married, the villein paid money to the lord. And when a villein died, his son had to give the lord the family's best ox or cow.

The village **reeve** made sure that each man did the right amount of work for the lord. If there was a quarrel between two peasants, it was settled in the lord of the manor's court. Men, or women, who had done wrong ended up in the village stocks. The same happened to reeves who did not do their jobs properly.

Freemen were better-off peasants. (There were a lot of freemen in the south-east of England.) They paid rent in money to the lord of the manor, but had to do little or no work on the lord's land. And they could leave the village if they wished.

Cottars and **bordars**, on the other hand, were worse off than villeins. They had far less land in the open fields, and earned money by working for wages on the lord's land. Like villeins and freemen, they could keep cattle and sheep on the common.

Now try Exercise 10.3.

Shepherds looking after the sheep on the common land.

Source 10b

In Boldon, there are 22 villeins. Each villein has 60 acres. He has to pay four shillings (20 pence) a year, and work three days a week for the lord. He does four extra 'boon days' at reaping time. He must give the lord two hens and ten eggs each year.

There are twelve cottars. Each of them has twelve acres. A cottar works two days a week.

From the records of the Bishops of Durham. This extract tells us about the manor of Boldon in Durham in the year 1183.

Source 10c

In Kettering there are 40 villeins. Each villein has about 30 acres of land. He has to work three days a week for the lord, and must plough four acres for the lord in the spring. He has to pay two shillings (10 pence) to the lord each year. And he must give the lord a hen at Christmas and 16 eggs at Easter.

There are eight cottars, and they have five acres of land each. A cottar works one day a week for the lord.

From the records of Peterborough Abbey. This extract tells us about the manor of Kettering in Northants in the year 1125.

This stone manor house was built at Boothby Pagnell in Lincolnshire in about 1200. Wooden manor houses, with thatched roofs were more common.

A reeve watching over the harvesting.

Exercise 10.3

Read **Section B** and **Sources 10b** and **10c**.
We can find out a lot from the sources if we ask the right questions. Try asking 'How many . . . ?' and 'How much . . . ?' about **Sources 10b** and **10c**. They are about two different parts of England. They show that the peasants were the same in some ways, and different in others.
Answer the questions. In each case, write one sentence about each manor, starting as shown in **a**.

a How many villeins were there?
  i In Boldon . . . .
  ii In Kettering . . . .
b How much land did a villein have?
c How much work did a villein do for the lord?
d How much money did a villein have to pay to the lord?
e How many hens and eggs did a villein have to give to the lord?
f How many cottars were there?
g How much land did cottars have, and how much work had they to do?

C How did things change?

The population of England rose steadily between 1066 and 1348. The extra people needed more food, and the chief food was bread. So the peasants had to plough more land, and grow more corn.

In some parts of England, they ploughed up part of the common land, and made extra fields. So now many villages had three open fields. The peasants still left one field fallow each year, but they grew crops in the other two. They still worked the fields in strips.

Money began to play a bigger part in the peasants' lives. Some lords stop-ped making villeins give them two or three days' work a week. They let them pay **rent** instead, like freemen. The lords' land still had to be worked, of course. So the lords paid **wages** to cottars, bordars, and poor villeins to work for them.

Some freemen and villeins became quite rich by selling corn in the market towns. (The more land they had, the more corn they grew.) So they rented extra land from their lords, and became richer still. Like the lords of the manor, they paid the poorer peasants to work for them.

Now try Exercises 10.4 and 10.5.

Exercise 10.4

Read **Section C**.
How much changed, and how much stayed the same?
Write four short paragraphs about the following. Say which things changed, and which did not change, in the lives of peasants between the eleventh century and the fourteenth century.

a The village, and how the peasants farmed the land.
b Work, rent, and wages.
c Rich peasants.
d Poor peasants.

Exercise 10.5

Write out the sentences below. Instead of the words in **bold print**, write 'In the .... century'. (Add the words 'early', 'mid', or 'late' if they are needed.)

a **In 1066**, the population of England was about two million.
b **Between 1071 and 1100**, a lot of villages had only two open fields.
c **In 1150**, peasants lived in wood and clay huts, with thatched roofs and earth floors.
d **Between 1171 and 1200**, peasants cut down a lot of trees and turned some forests into farm land.
e **Between 1201 and 1300**, many peasants started paying their rents in money.
f **Between 1301 and 1330**, rich peasants rented extra land from their lords.
g **In 1348**, the population of England was about five million.

11th century peasants

11 The Black Death and the Peasants' Revolt

A The Black Death

The 'Black Death' – a kind of plague – reached the ports of southern England in 1348. It swept through the country in the next year. Those who caught it died in a day or two, sometimes less. Between a third and a half of the people in England died. No-one knew what caused the Black Death, or how to cure it.

We know now that the plague was carried by black rats. It was spread to humans by the rats' fleas. The dirt and rubbish which lay in the streets of towns were ideal for the rats, so the towns were hit worst by the plague. London had special 'plague pits' for burying the dead.

When townspeople fled to the country to escape the disease, they took it with them. So many peasants died that there were not enough people left to till the fields. Whole villages were deserted, and the houses began to fall down.

Now try Exercise 11.1.

Exercise 11.1

Read **Section A** and **Sources 11a** and **11b**.

a Which **fact** is mentioned in **both Source 11a** and **Source 11b**?
b Write down *three* facts that are mentioned **only** in **Source 11a**.
c Write down *three* facts that are mentioned **only** in **Source 11b**.

The remains of the deserted village at Olney in Northamptonshire, seen from the air. Can you see where the village street use to be, and signs of the strips in the fields?

Source 11a

In 1349 the great plague spread through the whole world from south to north. It was so bad that hardly half the population remained alive. Towns that were once full of men were left empty. In the end there were not enough men left alive to bury the dead.

Written by Thomas Walsingham in about 1400.

Source 11b

In 1349 there was an outbreak of plague. Those who caught it died suddenly. At least a third of all the people in the world died. Men called penitents flogged themselves with leather whips, spiked with iron. They hoped that this might persuade God to stop the plague.

From Jean Froissart's *Chronicles*, written in about 1400.

B The Peasants' Revolt

The peasants who survived the Black Death asked for higher wages. Lords of the manor had to pay, or leave their land untilled. For a while the peasants were on top. Then the lords hit back. They tried to make the peasants work two or three days a week for them, without wages, as in the past. Then parliament passed a law which banned high wages for peasants.

The peasants did not like any of this. Nor did they like the poll tax which was charged in 1380 to help pay for a war with France. Complaints led to revolt. Angry peasants attacked manor houses and made bonfires with the lords' record books.

Rebels from Essex and Kent reached London in June 1381. They pulled down and burned the houses of the great lords and rich merchants. They killed foreign tradesmen. They even cut off the head of the Archbishop of Canterbury, whom they blamed for the new tax.

King Richard II, who was only fourteen years old, met the rebels at Smithfield, on the edge of London. A fight broke out there between the mayor of London and Wat Tyler, the peasants'

Rebels murder the Archbishop of Canterbury and other advisers of the king.

Source 11c

The revolt broke out because the peasants were so well off. The bad people did not like having to work for their lords. They said that when the world began there were no villeins and lords. A crack-brained priest called John Ball told them that they had a right to proper wages. More than once, the Archbishop of Canterbury arrested John Ball and put him in prison. He should have had him put to death at once.

Also from Jean Froissart's *Chronicles*.

Source 11d

The common people of Kent and Essex revolted. They were against the duke of Lancaster and the other great lords. The main cause was the heavy tax that had been passed. It hit the poor people very hard.

From the *Anonymous Chronicle*.

leader. The mayor drew his sword and cut Tyler down. The peasants might have killed the mayor and the king in revenge. Richard kept cool. He faced the rebels, told them he would see to their complaints, and asked them to go home.

The king broke his promise. As soon as the danger was over, his ministers sent soldiers to deal with the rebels. They put the leaders to death. They burned down the villages where the peasants had revolted. But it was not all loss – the hated poll tax was not charged again.

Now try Exercise 11.2 and 11.3.

Exercise 11.2

Read **Section B**, and **Sources 11c** and **11d**.

a What were the **causes** of the Peasants' Revolt according to **Section B**?

_____

_____

b What were the **causes** of the Peasants' Revolt according to the author of **Source 11c**?

_____

_____

c What were the **causes** of the Peasants' Revolt according to the author of **Source 11d**?

_____

_____

Exercise 11.3

a Write down all the **facts** you can find in **Source 11c**.

_____

_____

_____

b What were the **opinions** of the author of **Source 11c** on

  i The peasants? _____

_____

  ii John Ball? _____

_____

c Whose side was the author of **Source 11c** on – the lords' or the peasants'?
Which words in **Source 11c** tell us the answer?

_____

_____

d **Source 11d** tells us that the peasants in which counties rebelled?

_____

_____

e Whose side was the author of **Source 11d** on? – the lords' or the peasants'?
Which words in **Source 11d** tell us the answer?

_____

_____

C Peasants in the fifteenth century

The Peasants' Revolt was crushed in 1381. Life did get better, though, for the peasants in the next hundred years. Those who did best were the freemen and the richest villeins, who by now were called **yeomen**. Yeomen added to their own strips in the village fields by buying land from other peasants. Then they rented more land from the lords of the manor.

There were clear signs that the yeomen had money. They built new, bigger houses, sometimes in stone instead of wood and clay. They could afford better clothes and furniture. They kept servants. Some of them even sent their sons to school.

Times were better even for the poor peasants. (People had stopped using the name 'villein' by the year 1450.) They no longer had to do unpaid work for their lords. They had some land of their own, and they earned wages by working for the lords or the yeomen as well. And wages were quite high in the fifteenth century.

But peasants' lives were always hard. Their families were often hungry. The men (and often women as well) worked in the fields, six days a week, from dawn to dusk. The women also milked the cows and sheep, made butter and cheese, looked after the children, and cooked what food there was. Not many peasants lived to be more than fifty.

Now try Exercise 11.4.

This is a Welsh farmhouse from the Middle Ages. The family lived at one end, and the animals were kept at the other.

The interior of the Welsh farmhouse. It has been rebuilt in the Welsh Folk Museum.

Making up your mind

As you know, the sources contain different opinions about the past. And authors of history books do not all say the same thing.
How do you decide who is right?
The best idea always is to look at the **facts**. Ask, 'Do the facts show, or **prove**, that this opinion is right?'
There may be no facts to show that it is right. In that case, the opinion may be wrong.

Exercise 11.4

Read **Section C**, then study the following question.

Were yeomen the only peasants who were better off in the fifteenth century?

Now plan an answer to the question above.

a Write down any facts which show that yeomen were better off.
b Write down any facts which show that poor peasants were better off.
c Is it true that **only** yeomen were better off?

Source 11e

The mayor of London kills Wat Tyler. King Richard II is shown twice. The artist wanted to show that after Wat Tyler was killed, the king rode over to the peasants.

A fifteenth-century scene showing criminals in the stocks.

Source 11f

The mayor drew a great sword, struck at Wat Tyler, and laid him flat. The crowds began to mutter. 'They've killed our leader', they said. Then the king rode alone right up to those crazy people and said: 'What do you want? I am your king. I am your leader. Go home in peace'.

Also written by Jean Froissart.

Exercise 11.5

Look at **Source 11e** and read **Source 11f**.

a Which things can we learn from **both Source 11e and Source 11f**?
b Which things can we learn **only** from **Source 11e**?
c Which things can we learn **only** from **Source 11f**?
d What kind of things can we find out best from **picture sources** (paintings, portraits, drawings, tapestries, etc.)?
  What kind of things can picture sources **not** normally tell us?
  Draw a chart to show what we can learn from picture sources (paintings, drawings, tapestries etc.) and what can we learn **only** from written sources?

A How warfare changed

War was part of normal life for Norman kings and lords. Princes and young nobles had to learn to ride and fight as knights. Barons, earls, and bishops, with their knights, had to fight for the king when he needed them. This was how they paid the rent for their land.

Three hundred years later, kings and lords still went to war. And knights were still the main troops in the army. But there were some changes. Norman knights wore chainmail. By the fourteenth century, though, knights' armour had some solid plates of steel. In the fifteenth, they wore full suits of armour.

The Normans had archers, armed with short bows. From the year 1300, there were always archers with **longbows** in the English army. Longbows were two metres long, and could shoot arrows right through plate armour. By 1350, there were also some guns. But they often did more damage to their own side than the enemy.

In the fourteenth and fifteenth centuries, kings needed a lot of money to fight wars. Each of the great lords had his private army, and soldiers had to be paid wages. So the king gave money to the great lords, and they paid wages to the soldiers.

Now try Exercise 12.1

Source 12a

Knights sometimes fought on foot in the fourteenth and fifteenth centuries. When they did so they were called 'men-at-arms'.

Source 12b

A knight's lady hands him his helmet.

Source 12c

A fifteenth-century suit of armour

Source 12d

Some of the weapons used by men-at-arms.

Exercise 12.1

Read **Section A**, and look at **Sources 12a**, **12b**, **12c**, and **12d**. Which things changed between the eleventh century and the fourteenth and fifteenth centuries? Fill in the blank spaces in the chart below. In the column headed '**Change?**', write either **Change** or **No Change**.

11th Century	14th & 15th Centuries	Change?
Kings led their armies into battle.	_____ led their armies into _____	_____
Knights were the most important soldiers.	_____ were the most important soldiers.	_____
Knights wore armour made of chain-mail.	Knights wore _____ _____	_____
Archers with short bows fought in the army.	Archers with _____ _____	_____
The great lords paid rent for their land by sending knights to help the king.	The king paid _____ _____ _____	_____
There were no guns.	_____	

© Oxford University Press

B The Hundred Years' War

England's longest war was against France. It lasted, with a few breaks, from 1336 to 1453, and was called the 'Hundred Years' War'. It began when King **Edward III** said that he had a right to be king of France.

Edward and his son, the **Black Prince**, won some famous victories. Edward beat the French at **Crécy** in 1346, and took the town of **Calais** the next year. In 1356, the Black Prince beat the French king at **Poitiers**. But when the Black Prince and Edward died, the French began to win battles. By 1400, the English had only a few towns around the French coast.

Henry V began the war again in 1415. He took the town of Harfleur in Normandy, then beat a large French army at **Agincourt**. Henry was a hero to his men and all the people of England.

King **Charles VI** of France made peace in 1420. He said that Henry would become king of France when he, Charles VI, died. Henry married Charles's daughter, and a son was born in 1421. But the prince was only nine months old when Henry V died. Charles VI died six weeks later. The English said that the baby (**Henry VI**) was now king of England and France.

Now try Exercise 12.2.

The 'burghers' of Calais kneel before Edward III.

 Source 12f

Edward agreed that if six men of Calais surrendered to him, he would spare the rest. They had to come out with their heads and feet bare, ropes round their necks, and the keys of the town in their hands. Edward said their heads were to be cut off straight away. But the queen begged him on her knees to spare them. So the king gave way and let them go.

From Jean Froissart's *Chronicles*.

 Source 12e

The siege of Calais lasted for a whole year. The people were so hungry that they ate all the horses, dogs, and cats. At last, the captain and his chief men came out without hats or shoes, and with ropes round their necks. They gave Edward the keys of the town and begged him not to kill them. He said he would spare their lives, and sent them to the Tower of London.

From a book written by a monk in York in the fourteenth century.

Exercise 12.2

Read **Section B**, then read **Sources 12e** and **12f**.

a Write down *three* facts mentioned in **Source 12e**, but **not** in **Source 12f**.
b Write down *three* facts mentioned in **Source 12f**, but **not** in **Source 12e**.
c Which facts are mentioned by **both** sources?

C Joan of Arc and the end of the war

Charles VI of France had a son (another Charles). Men called him the **Dauphin**, which was always the title of the French kings' eldest son. When Charles VI died, some Frenchmen fought on for the Dauphin. They did not have much hope, for he was a weak and idle youth.

Then **Joan of Arc** appeared. Joan was a peasant girl from Domrémy in eastern France. She said that she had heard voices and seen visions of the saints. The voices told her to go to the Dauphin at the castle of **Chinon** and help him to save **Orléans** from the English.

The courtiers at Chinon laughed at Joan. But the Dauphin gave her arms, and sent her with 4,000 men to relieve Orléans (make the English give up the siege). Joan beat the English in battle, and drove them back to the north. The Dauphin was crowned King Charles VII in Rheims cathedral.

Then Joan was captured by the duke of Burgundy (England's ally), and put on trial by the English. They said she was a **witch** – she had seen and talked to devils. She was found guilty and burned to death in the market-place at **Rouen** in May 1431.

Killing Joan of Arc did not save the English. As Henry VI grew up, it was clear that he was not a soldier. In any case, England could not afford the long war and lost its chief ally, the duke of Burgundy. In 1453, the French took Bordeaux, and the war was over. **Calais** was the only part of France left in English hands.

Now try Exercise 12.3.

The French, commanded by Joan of Arc, attack Paris (which was held by the English).

France in the Time of Henry V and Joan of Arc

London
ENGLAND
Calais
FLANDERS
Agincourt
GERMANY
English Channel
Harfleur
Rouen
Rheims
NORMANDY
Paris
Domrémy
Orléans
Chinon
BURGUNDY
Bordeaux
GASCONY

N W E S

0   100   200   300
Km

Land Controlled by

the Dauphin in 1429   the King of England in 1429   the Duke of Burgundy in 1429

Exercise 12.3

Read **Section C**.
Write sentences to show that you know what these words mean:

a Dauphin   d Siege
b Vision   e Relieve
c Courtiers   f Witch

Source 12g

The French army was crowded together between two small woods. The knights hardly had room to raise their lances. It had rained all night, and the ground was too soft for the horses. The heavy armour worn by the French knights made things worse.

The English knights were on foot and advanced in good order. The archers were at the sides of the field. When they fired, the arrows fell so fast that the French did not dare look up. When the English knights reached them, many of them had already been killed or wounded. The men at the back of the French army saw what was happening and ran away.

Jean de Waurin's account of the Battle of Agincourt in 1415. Jean fought as a knight on the French side in the battle.

Source 12h

The men of Orléans badly needed Joan's help, for they had begun to give up hope. They greeted her well. The troops promised to follow her, and she led them out to attack the English. They won one victory after another. Then men said she had been sent by God, and that nothing could stop them.

Adapted from a book written by Sir Charles Oman in 1895.

Source 12i

The English were short of men and money. They never had much hope of taking Orléans. They only had a weak hold on northern France. Joan did not need to be a great general or to have God's help to relieve Orléans and capture other towns.

Adapted from a book written by Dr. A. R. Myers in 1952.

Exercise 12.4

Read **Source 12g**.

a Is **Source 12g** a primary or a secondary source? (Write a sentence, giving your opinion and your reason.)
b What were the **causes** of the English victory at Agincourt? (Write down a list of causes.)
c Which was the most important cause of the English victory? (Write a paragraph, giving your opinions and your reasons.)

Exercise 12.5

Read **Sources 12h** and **12i**, then answer the questions.
Write at least one sentence in answer to each question.

a The siege of Orléans:
  i What does **Source 12h** say about Orléans before Joan arrived?
  ii What does **Source 12i** say about the siege of Orléans?
b Joan as a general:
  i What does **Source 12h** say to make you think that Joan was a good general?
  ii What does **Source 12i** say about Joan as a general?
c God's help:
  i What does **Source 12h** say about God's help for Joan?
  ii What does **Source 12i** say about God's help for Joan?

Exercise 12.6

Read the story of Joan of Arc in Section B again. Which do you think are the three most important events in the story? Write your own notes saying what happened and why the events were important **or** make a tape.

13 Lancaster, York, and Tudor

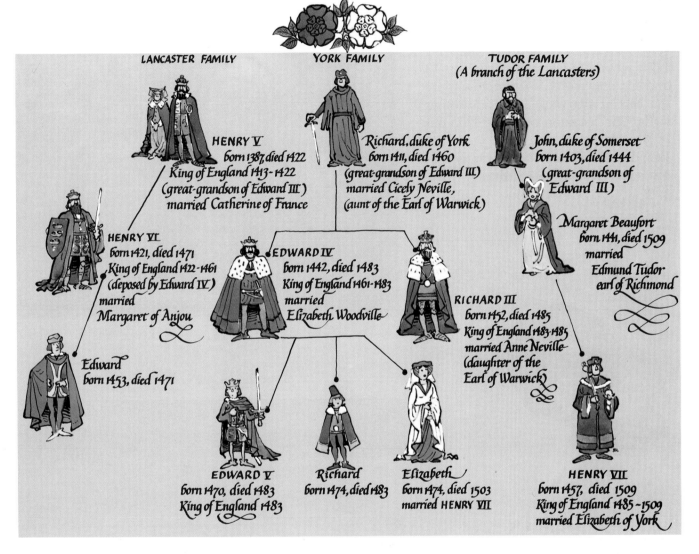

LANCASTER FAMILY

YORK FAMILY

TUDOR FAMILY
(A branch of the Lancasters)

HENRY V
born 1387, died 1422
King of England 1413-1422
(great-grandson of Edward III)
married Catherine of France

Richard, duke of York
born 1411, died 1460
(great-grandson of Edward III)
married Cicely Neville,
(aunt of the Earl of Warwick)

John, duke of Somerset
born 1403, died 1444
(great-grandson of
Edward III)

HENRY VI
born 1421, died 1471
King of England 1422-1461
(deposed by Edward IV)
married
Margaret of Anjou

EDWARD IV
born 1442, died 1483
King of England 1461-1483
married
Elizabeth Woodville

RICHARD III
born 1452, died 1485
King of England 1483-1485
married Anne Neville
(daughter of the
Earl of Warwick)

Margaret Beaufort
born 1441, died 1509
married
Edmund Tudor
earl of Richmond

Edward
born 1453, died 1471

EDWARD V
born 1470, died 1483
King of England 1483

Richard
born 1474, died 1483

Elizabeth
born 1474, died 1503
married HENRY VII

HENRY VII
born 1457, died 1509
King of England 1485-1509
married Elizabeth of York

A The Wars of the Roses

Henry VI could not win the war in France. He could not keep the peace in England either. Each lord had a band of men who wore his badge. They stole from the people, and beat them up if they complained. The courts were no help – the lords' men bullied the judges and juries as well.

The greatest nobles had private armies. When they fell out with each other in the 1450s, there was civil war. One group, led by Henry VI's wife, **Queen Margaret**, fought to keep Henry on the throne, and make sure that their son was the next king. Their enemies thought that England would be better off with **Richard, duke of York**, in charge.

The two sides were called **Lancaster** (the king's family) and **York**. The wars between them are known as the **Wars of the Roses**. (The captions below tell you why.) Most nobles took one side or the other. The greatest lord in England, the **earl of Warwick**, was on the side of York at first.

The York family won the wars, but Duke Richard was killed in battle. His son, **Edward IV**, became king. By 1471, when the wars ended, Henry VI and his son were dead, and so were the earl of Warwick and many other lords. The common people stayed out of the fighting – the wars were not their business. But while they lasted, there was no real law and order.

Now try Exercise 13.1.

King Edward IV (seated), with the queen and their son, the future Edward V, standing on his left. Kneeling before the king is William Caxton, who published the first books to be printed in England.

The Red Rose of Lancaster

The White Rose of York

The Red Rose was the badge of the Lancaster side, and the White Rose was the badge of the York side.

Exercise 13.1

Read **Section A**, and study the family trees. Write your answers to the questions in the spaces.

a How old was Henry VI when he became a king? _____

b Who was Henry VI's wife? _____

c For how many years was Henry VI king of England? _____

d How old was Henry VI's son when he died? _____

e Who was the duke of York's wife? _____

f How old was Edward IV when he became king? _____

g For how many years was Edward IV king of England? ____

B The princes in the Tower

Edward IV died in 1483, aged only forty-one. His two sons were twelve and nine years old. The elder of them was now **King Edward V**, but he was too young to rule. His uncle **Richard, duke of Gloucester,** became 'Protector', to govern England until the boy-king grew up.

In less than three months, the Protector had made himself **King Richard III**. The two 'princes' (Edward V and his brother) were put in the Tower of London 'to be safe'. Rumours soon spread that they were dead. They were never seen again.

Did Richard III have his nephews killed? No-one really knows. Richard had a good reason to get rid of the princes – each of them had more right to be king than he did. Their own mother was sure that they were dead. And if they **were** put to death in the Tower, Richard would have known about it.

A revolt against Richard broke out in October 1483. One of the causes was the rumour that the princes had been killed. Richard could have crushed the rumour and the revolt by letting people see the princes, alive and well. He did not. Does this mean that they were dead?

One last fact came to light nearly 200 years later. In 1674, some workmen found the bones of two children in the Tower of London. Experts who examined the bones in 1933 said that they belonged to two boys, aged about twelve and nine.

Now try Exercises 13.2 and 13.3.

This stained-glass window in Canterbury Cathedral shows the two princes in the Tower'. Richard is on the left and Edward is on the right.

Exercise 13.2

Read **Section B**, then answer the questions.

a Do **you** think that the princes were murdered? (Write a sentence.)
b Do **you** think that Richard III ordered someone to murder the princes? (Write a sentence.)
c **Why** might Richard III have ordered someone to murder the princes? (Write one or two sentences.)
d Which of the facts given in **Section B** make Richard III look guilty?
e Did the discovery of the bones **prove** that Richard III was guilty? (Write at least one sentence, giving your reasons.)

Richard III – notes about the sources

a Sources written in Richard III's lifetime did not say that he murdered the princes. They said that there was a **rumour** that they had been killed. No-one ever confessed to the crime.

b Sir Thomas More wrote a book about Richard III in 1520 (35 years after Richard's death). He said that Richard got a man called James Tyrrel to go to the Tower with two murderers. Tyrrel and his men, More said, smothered the princes with their own bedclothes.

c William Shakespeare, who wrote his play *Richard III* in 1593, more than a hundred years after Richard's time, told the same story as Sir Thomas More. In the play, we hear Richard telling Tyrrel to kill the princes.

The badge worn by supporters of the earl of Warwick.

Exercise 13.3

Think again

Sometimes, new facts should make you think again.
Read 'Richard III – notes about the sources'. Some people say that there is no **proof** that Richard III murdered the princes. There were **rumours** that he had done so, but no more. After Richard's death, the rumours were turned into a legend.

Now read again your answers to Exercise 13.2. Do you still think the same? Or do you think you were too hard on Richard III? (There is nothing wrong with changing your mind, or saying that you are not sure.) Write a paragraph, saying how your ideas have changed, and why. If they have not changed, give your reasons.

C Henry VII, the first Tudor king of England

Richard III reigned for only two years. He was popular in the north, where he had lived as a young man. But he was not liked in the south. He made things worse by giving top jobs in the south to his northern friends.

Henry Tudor, earl of Richmond, was now the chief hope of Richard's enemies. Henry's mother was one of the last of the Lancasters. His father was a half-Welsh lord. When Henry landed in Wales from France in August 1485 with a small army, a lot of Welshmen joined him.

Richard met the invaders at **Bosworth** near Leicester on 22 August. Richard had the bigger army, but not all his men were loyal. He lost the battle, and his life. Henry, earl of Richmond, became **Henry VII**, England's first **Tudor** king.

Henry VII knew that England needed peace, law and order. There must be an end to civil war. He put some supporters of Richard III to death, and kept others in prison. But he hoped there would be friendship in the future between York and Lancaster. That is why he married Elizabeth, Richard's niece.

Henry banned private armies. Lords who disobeyed him had to pay big fines. Those who rebelled against him lost their lands. The money and lands made Henry so rich that he did not need to ask the lords for help.

Now try Exercise 13.4.

Exercise 13.4

Read **Section C**, then answer the questions in sentences.

a What was Henry Tudor's **motive** or **reason** when he landed in Wales in 1485?
b What was Henry VII's **motive** for putting some of Richard III's supporters to death?
c What was Henry VII's **motive** for marrying Elizabeth of York?
d What was Henry VII's **motive** for banning private armies?
e What were Henry VII's **motives** for taking money and land from lords who were against him? (Try to think of more than one motive.)

Source 13a

He is more popular with the people than any king was before. As he travels around, he does good to the poor. He refuses gifts of money offered by the cities and towns. God has sent him to help us.

Part of a letter written in the reign of Richard III by Thomas Langton, the bishop of St. David's in Wales.)

Source 13b

A portrait of King Richard III

Source 13c

A wood-carving of King Richard III in Christchurch, Dorset.

Source 13d

Richard was a little man, with a crooked back. His left shoulder was much higher than his right. He had a hard face and a cruel look. He was bad-tempered, envious, and dishonest. He pretended to be friendly to men he was planning to kill. They say that with his own hands he killed King Henry VI when he was a prisoner in the Tower.

From Sir Thomas More's *History of Richard III*, written in about 1520.

Exercise 13.5

Look at **Sources 13b** and **13c**, and read **Sources 13a** and **13d**. Note down the answers to these questions. Then discuss your answers in a group.

a What does **Source 13d** say about Richard III's appearance?
b What does **Source 13c** tell us about Richard III's appearance? Does it tell us the same things as **Source 13d**?
c What does **Source 13b** tell us about Richard III's appearance? Does it tell us the same things as **Source 13d**?
d What does **Source 13d** say about Richard III's character?
e What does **Source 13a** say about Richard III's character?
f Why do you think the sources say different things about Richard III? Do you think that any of them show bias, either against Richard, or in favour of Richard?

14 Towns and Trade

A The Main Towns in England in About 1180

SCOTLAND

Newcastle
Carlisle

York

Chester · Lincoln
Stafford
Shrewsbury · Leicester Norwich
Warwick · Thetford
WALES Worcester Northampton · Cambridge
· Oxford · Ipswich
· Bristol · London
Winchester · Canterbury
Lewes ·
· Launceston

One of London's town gates with town walls beyond

A The towns

Most people lived in villages in the Middle Ages, and did not often leave home. When they did go to town, they had to walk – up to ten miles (16 kilometres) each way.

Every town had a market. Peasants' main reason for going to town was to buy and sell there. They sold the eggs, cheese, wool, or corn they had brought with them. And they spent the few pence they made on the things they could not grow or make – shoes, cloth, pots and pans.

There were no big shops or factories in the towns. The only shops, apart from the market stalls, were the front rooms of craftsmen's houses. Customers stepped straight from the narrow, dirty streets into the workshops.

Most townspeople were part-time farmers. There were fields and common land outside every town, and gardens inside the walls. Some families kept animals in their homes. Hens and pigs searched for food in the heaps of refuse in the streets.

London was the biggest town in England. About 10,000 people lived there in 1066. Like other towns, it grew in the twelfth and thirteenth centuries. Even so, it was just a cluster of streets on the north bank of the Thames, between the Tower of London and Fleet Street. Rich merchants and great lords owned the only stone houses.

Now try Exercise 14.1.

(B) **Towns in England in the 14ᵗʰ Century**

SCOTLAND

Newcastle ⊙

York ⊚   Beverley
         · Hull

         Lincoln
Newark ⊙   Boston ⊙
Nottingham ·   King's Lynn ⊚   Great Yarmouth ⊙
Shrewsbury ·   Stamford ⊙   Norwich ⊙
Peterborough ·   Ely ·
Coventry ⊙
WALES   Hereford ·   Cambridge ·   · Bury St Edmunds
Gloucester ·   Oxford ⊙   · Luton   · Ipswich
Bristol ⊚   Newbury ·   ▣ London
Salisbury ⊙   · Winchester   · Canterbury
· Exeter   · Southampton
Plymouth ·

Key: Population

▣ Over 50,000   ⊙ 5,000 to 10,000

⊚ 10,000 to 20,000   · 2,500 to 5,000

The population figures are estimates, based on the amount of tax each town paid in 1334

Exercise 14.1

Read **Section A**, and look at **Maps A** and **B**. Answer the questions. Write your answers in the spaces.

a How many people lived in London:

   i in the eleventh century?

   _____

   ii in the fourteenth century?

   _____

b In which part of England were there most towns in 1180 (south-east, south-west, midlands, north)?

   _____

c Which of these towns are shown on **B**, but *not* on **A**? (York, Southampton, Bristol, Newcastle, Boston, King's Lynn, Oxford)

   _____

d Why do you think these towns are not shown on **Map A**? _____

   _____

e Study **Map B** carefully, then complete the chart below by writing in the names of the towns.

Population of towns in the fourteenth century			
Over 50,000 people	10,000 to 20,000 people	5,000 to 10,000 people	2,500 to 5,000 people
....	....	....	....
	....	....	....
		....	....
		....	....
		....	....
			....
			....

B Merchants and craftsmen

This wine jug from France was found in the remains of a 13th century merchant's house in Southampton. It proves that English merchants imported French wine at that time.

The most important persons in a town were the merchants. They fixed the taxes to be paid by people coming into the town to sell goods. They set the laws for the markets. They tried to make sure that no-one cheated or stole.

Merchants were traders who got rich by buying and selling goods. They bought wool, corn, and skins from country people. Then they sold them at a profit, sometimes to traders from abroad at trade **fairs**. These were big markets, where merchants met to buy and sell their goods.

Craftsmen were skilled workers. They made shoes, pots, swords, hats, etc. The most important of them were the men who owned the workshops. They were called the **masters**. But each craftsman began as an **apprentice**, living in the master's house and learning in his shop. When he was old enough and skilled enough, he became a **journeyman**. Now he worked for real wages, paid by the master. Every journeyman hoped one day to be a master.

By the thirteenth century, each town had a **guild** for each of the main trades. And the craftsmen had to belong to the guilds. (All the stocking-makers in York had to belong to the York hosiers' guild. All the leather-makers in Newcastle were in the Newcastle tanners' guild.)

A group of masters was in charge of each guild. They said how the goods should be made and what the prices should be. They made rules about what the apprentices had to learn. They gave money to members who were ill, and paid pensions to the widows of members who had died. The masters of most guilds were men, but some (such as the silk-makers of London) were women.

Now try Exercise 14.2.

Two craftsmen being tested by their Guild Master.

Exercise 14.2

Read **Section B**. Write your own notes on **guilds**. Use your own words.

a Say what a guild was.
b Give two examples of guilds.
c Say which men were in charge of guilds.
d Say what kind of rules guilds made.
e Say what guilds did to look after their members and their families.

C The wool and cloth trade

English wool was the best in Europe. Lords and abbots kept huge flocks of sheep, and the wool made them rich. **Wool-merchants**, who bought and sold wool, had big houses and wore fine clothes. The richest men in London were those who sold wool to the cloth-makers of **Flanders** (modern Belgium). Even the king borrowed money from the wool-merchants.

Before the fourteenth century, **woollen cloth** was made in the towns. After that, a lot of the work was done by village people. Rich **clothiers** in the towns bought raw wool from the wool-merchants. Then they sent it by packhorse out to the villages. Peasants spun the yarn and wove the cloth in their homes. The clothiers paid their wages.

Most English people had always dressed in English-made cloth. But not much English cloth was sold abroad – it was not good enough. Then, soon after the year 1300, there was a change. English cloth improved, and clothiers started selling it in Flanders, France, and Spain. Exports of wool fell, and exports of cloth grew.

Cloth-making did not make the peasants rich. But it made the fortunes of the wool-merchants and clothiers. You can still see clothiers' houses in towns like Colchester and Chipping Campden. And in many parts of England there are churches that were rebuilt with wool-merchants' money.

Now try Exercise 14.3.

Dyers in the Middle Ages dying cloth.

Lavenham Church – work on the new tower began in 1490. It was paid for by the rich clothiers of the town.

Exercise 14.3

Read **Section C**. Which things changed, and which things stayed the same? Write your own notes about the following:

a Wool exports.
b Cloth-making.
c Cloth exports.
d The quality of English wool.
e Merchants' profits.

Source 14a

King Henry III takes all the food, drink, and clothing he needs, by force, from the merchants. To save themselves, they have gone into hiding. Foreign merchants will not come to England. So trade has been brought to a stop. The king does not even let the poor fishermen sell their herrings as they want. They dare not come ashore for fear of being robbed.

Written by a monk called Matthew Paris in 1248.

Source 14b

You officers of the law should put dishonest brewers, bakers, butchers, and cooks in your pillories and ducking-stools. These are the men who do most harm to the poor. They poison them with bad food, and over-charge them. They grow rich by robbing the poor. How could they build such tall houses, and buy up land and farms, if they were honest?

From *Piers Ploughman*, a poem written by William Langland in about 1380.

Source 14c

I have been round all the drapers' shops in this town (Norwich), and I can't buy any cloth good enough for a dress. Everything is too simple in colour and quality. Would you please get me three yards and a quarter of something you think would suit me? Choose whatever colour you like.

A letter from Margaret Paston to her husband, who was in London, in 1465. The Pastons were quite rich landowners in Norfolk.

Source 14d

I am giving you five shillings (25 pence) to buy sugar and dates for me. Please send them as soon as you can. Let me know the price per pound of pepper, cloves, mace, ginger, cinnamon, almonds, rice, and raisins. If these things are cheaper in London than they are here, I shall send you the money to buy them.

A letter from Margaret Paston to her son, who was in London, in 1471.

Exercise 14.4

Read **Sources 14a** and **14b**, then answer the questions.

a Write down three **facts** from **Source 14a**.
b What was Matthew Paris's **opinion** of Henry III?
c Which words show that Matthew Paris was sorry for the fishermen?
d **Source 14b** says that 'dishonest' tradesmen have done what?
e **Source 14b** says that the tradesmen have spent their money on what?
f Whose side do you think the author of **Source 14b** was on?

Exercise 14.5

Read **Sources 14c** and **14d**. Answer questions a and b in sentences, and questions c to e in paragraphs.

a Who wrote **Sources 14c** and **14d**, and when?
b Are **Sources 14c** and **14d** primary or secondary sources? (Give a reason for your opinion.)
c What do **Sources 14c** and **14d** tell us about the clothes and food that the Pastons liked?
d What do **Sources 14c** and **14d** tell us about the shops in Norwich and London?
e Do you think that most families in the fifteenth century were like the Pastons? Do **Sources 14c** and **14d** tell us how most men and women did their shopping? (Give your reasons.)

15 Technology in the Middle Ages

'**Technology**' means the right tools or equipment to do a job, and knowing how to use them. Technology may be advanced, like the computer. Or it may be simple, like the windmill or the spinning wheel.

A Builders

We can still see the castles, cathedrals, and churches of the Middle Ages. We admire their high stone walls, towers, and huge windows filled with coloured glass. Their carved stone **vaults** carried higher and wider roofs than anyone had built before. The **masons** who built them were skilled craftsmen and artists.

Source 15a shows how masons worked. Their scaffolding was made from wooden poles roped together. Men pulled the heavy stones up with ropes and pulleys. For arches and vaults, they first made a wooden frame, then set the stones in the frame and cemented them together.

The masons were bands of craftsmen who travelled from job to job. Cathedrals took years to build. Some were built and rebuilt more than once. Not all the buildings were perfect – walls sometimes collapsed. Many a mason lost his life in an accident.

Now try Exercise 15.1.

Source 15a

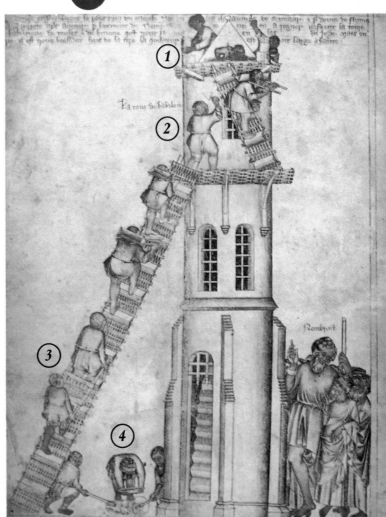

Masons working on a tower.

Exercise 15.1

Read **Section A**, and look at **Source 15a**.
The four building workers in **Source 15a** have been marked with numbers. Write a sentence about each of them, saying what you think the person is doing and what tools are being used (if any).

B Mills

In 1086, there were more than 5,000 **water-mills** in England. A water-mill used the village stream to turn a great wooden wheel. This turned the stone that milled the flour. But water-mills could do more than grind corn. They were used by cloth-makers and iron-workers (see Sections C and D). Water power even helped to make paper.

The first **windmills** were built in England just before the year 1200. A windmill was useful if there was no stream to drive a water-wheel. It worked only if the sails faced the wind, but the wind does not always blow from the same direction.

Technology's answer was a windmill that moved to face the wind. The whole mill turned to and fro on a huge wooden post fixed into the ground. That is why they were called 'post-mills'. Unlike water-mills, windmills were only used for grinding corn.

Now try Exercise 15.2.

Source 15b

Herbert the dean set up a windmill. When the abbot heard about this, he got so angry that he could hardly eat or speak. He ordered his servants to pull the mill down straight away. But the dean said he had a right to have a mill on his own land. He said any man had a right to use the wind. He also said that the mill was to grind his own corn and no-one else's. But the abbot had his way and the mill was pulled down.

Written by a monk at Bury St. Edmunds in 1191.

A windmill

Exercise 15.2

Read **Section B**, and read **Source 15b**.

a Who set up the windmill (**Source 15b**) and who objected?

_____

_____

b What was the abbot's opinion about the windmill?

_____

c The dean's opinion was that he had which two rights?

_____

_____

d What promise did the dean make?

_____

e Can you guess **why** the abbot was so angry? (Write a sentence.)

_____

_____

_____

C Cloth-making

Making woollen cloth was England's main industry in the Middle Ages. Wool from the sheep was **combed**, then **spun** into thread or yarn. (Women used spindle and distaff to pull and twist the wool.) Next, the **weaver**, on a loom, turned the yarn into cloth. After that, the **fullers**, or 'walkers', trod and shrank the cloth in troughs of water to make it thicker and more solid. Finally, the cloth was **dyed** and finished.

There were two big steps forward in the Middle Ages. **Fulling mills** began to do the work that walkers had done. They used water-wheels to drive hammers, which beat the cloth as it lay in the troughs of water. Soon after, the **spinning-wheel** started to take the place of the spindle and distaff. Technology was slowly changing.

Combing, spinning and weaving

Water mills like this were used for fulling from the thirteenth century onwards.

D The iron industry and the printing press

In the Middle Ages, ploughs, knives, spades, and scythes all had iron blades. Horses needed iron shoes, held on by iron nails. Spears and arrows had iron heads. Knights wore iron armour. The best swords were steel, which is made mainly from iron.

Miners dug **iron ore** from the ground, then **smelters** used charcoal-burning furnaces to extract iron from the ore. **Blacksmiths** worked, or wrought, the iron – they heated it to make it soft, then hammered it into the right shapes. Every village had its smith.

After about the year 1300, some smiths used water-wheels to drive the bellows which blew air into their furnaces. A mechanical bellows meant a much hotter furnace, so the iron could be melted and poured into **moulds**. The objects made this way were called **cast iron**. The guns that were used in the wars after 1350 had cast-iron barrels.

In the Middle Ages, books were written out slowly by hand, often by monks. They were expensive because they took such a long time to make. So monasteries took great care of the books in their libraries.

Books became cheaper when **printing** began. The Chinese invented printing in the eleventh century. But no books were printed in Europe until 1445. **William Caxton**, who learned how to print in Germany and Flanders, published England's first printed books in 1477. After that, more books were on sale, and more people learned to read. One result was that news and ideas spread more quickly.

Now try Exercise 15.3.

An early printing press

Exercise 15.3

Change
Read **Sections C** and **D** on pages 77 and 78.
Look at the chart, 'Technology in the Middle Ages', then answer the questions in sentences.

a What change in castle-building happened in the twelfth century?
b When did cathedrals begin to have larger windows, with coloured glass?
c Where were there windmills before they reached England?
d What kind of mills were there in England in the eleventh and twelfth centuries?
e Which job in the cloth-making industry did not change much in the Middle Ages?
f In which century were water-mills first used in the iron industry? What were they used for?
g In which century was the printing press invented?

Technology in the Middle Ages

Date (AD)	1000	1100	1200	1300	1400

Building
Castles
● Normans built wood and earth castles
● Stone castles
● Chimneys instead of open hearths
● Glass windows

Cathedrals & Churces
● Normans built new stone cathedrals and churches with vaults
● Larger windows with coloured glass

Mills
Water mills used throughout the Middle Ages
● Windmills in France
● First windmills in England

Cloth-making
Spinning
Spinners used distaff and spindle
● Spinners began using spinning wheel

Weaving
Weaving done on a handloom throughout the Middle Ages

Fulling
Fulling done by walkers
● Water driven fulling mill

Iron Industry
Wrought iron
Smiths made iron objects by hand
● Some smiths began using mechanical hammer (water power)

Cast iron
No cast iron before 1350
● Mechanical bellows (cast iron began)

Other Technologies
● Ship's compass
● Mechanical clock
● Water-powered paper mills
● Ship's rudder
● Guns first used
● Printing press
● More coal needed – bigger, deeper coal mines

Exercise 15.4

The invention of the printing press was a very important step forward in technology. What were its results?

The sentences below have been split in half. Join together the halves that fit, and write out the complete sentences.

First half

- Monks could spend their time on other work because . . .
- Books became more plentiful and cheaper because . . .
- More people were able to own books because . . .
- More people wanted to learn to read because . . .
- There were soon more schools because . . .
- Men and women learned more about the outside world because . . .

Second half

- they were cheaper to buy
- parents realised that reading and writing were important.
- they were not needed to copy out books by hand.
- they could read about it in books.
- they could now afford to buy books, and wanted to be able to read them.
- it took much less time to produce them.

Source 15c

The master of the works says that the builders were paid higher wages than they were due. One of them got a fortnight's wages when he was absent and had done no work. The men got too much money for drink. Wood and stone had been taken away, and no-one knew where it went. The workmen often quarrelled, so that the work was delayed or done carelessly. The carpenter is an old man and cannot work in high places.

A report on the work going on at York Minster in 1345.

Source 15d

The nave of York Minster. This is the part of the minster that was being built in 1345, when Source 15c was written.

Exercise 15.5

Read **Source 15c**, and look at **Source 15d**.
Note down the answers to these questions. Then discuss these answers in a group.

a   Who wrote **Source 15c**, and when?
b   What was the author's **opinion** of the building workers?
c   The men mentioned in **Source 15c** were working on which part of York Minster? (Look at the caption to **Source 15d**.)
d   Describe what you can see in **Source 15d**.
e   Does **Source 15d** make you disbelieve **Source 15c**? Is it possible to believe both sources?
f   Why should we not always believe written sources?

The members of the group should tell the rest of the class what they think, either in short talks or by making a tape.

16 Daily Life

A Houses and furniture

Peasant families lived in one-room or two-room shacks. The shacks were made of wood, turf, and clay. The roofs were thatched. Fires burned in the centre of the earth floors. There were no chimneys, and there was no glass in the windows. In winter, the animals lived under the same roof as the people.

In the twelfth century, lords' houses were the same as peasants', only bigger. But by the year 1450, the **manor house** had become much grander. It was built of stone, and had tiled floors and glass windows. There were extra rooms for the lord and his family, and there was a separate kitchen, with a stone chimney.

Town houses were built in streets, and they were quite narrow. Rich merchants and master-craftsmen built extra storeys. The shop was on the ground floor, the family lived upstairs, and the servants slept in the attics. Often, the upper floors hung over the street.

Peasants' furniture was as simple as their houses. They had a trestle table, a few stools, and a chest to keep things in. They slept on straw mattresses on the floor. Even manor houses had only one chair. But lords and merchants had wooden beds with curtains, and tapestries to hang on the walls.

Now try Exercise 16.1.

A merchant's house in Exeter, built in the fourteenth century.

Exercise 16.1

Read **Section A**.

Why do we know so little about peasants' houses in the Middle Ages? Some reasons are printed below.

Decide which *you* think are the *five* most important reasons.

Write out your five reasons in order, with the most important first. If you can think of some reasons of your own, write them down as well.

a No-one has looked for remains of peasants' homes.
b Peasants' houses were made of wood and clay, so they soon fell down.
c The sources did not describe peasants' houses.
d Peasants often pulled their own houses down, and built new ones.
e No-one wants to live in peasants' cottages today.
f There are no TV programmes about peasants' houses.
g Cottages had no chimneys, so many of them burned down.
h Peasants lived in the country, and most people now live in the town.

B Clothes

The rich wore smart clothes made from fine wool, linen, velvet, silk, or fur. Both sexes liked bright colours. Lords and ladies had their clothes decorated with gold and silver thread, jewels, and fancy buttons.

Ladies' dresses were always long. (**Sources 16b** and **16c** show you how fashions changed.) Their heads were kept covered, and in the fifteenth century they wore large, heavy head-dresses. Between 1450 and 1500, the well-dressed man wore a very short tunic and bright hose (or tights). Sometimes the hose had different-coloured legs.

Peasants' clothes were made from coarse woollen or linen cloth. Many of them kept warm by wearing sheepskin or leather jackets. They dressed in dull colours – grey, dark brown, or dark green. Some could not afford shoes.

Now try Exercise 16.2.

Source 16a

Peasants' clothing from the fourteenth century

Source 16b

Fifteenth-century men's and women's fashions

Source 16c

Eleventh-century ladies costumes

Exercise 16.2

Read **Section B** and look at **Sources 16a**, **16b** and **16c**. Do any *one* of the following:

a Describe the changes in women's costume between the eleventh and fifteenth centuries.
b Describe a fourteenth-century peasant's clothes.
c Describe fifteenth-century men's fashion.

Write a paragraph and draw a picture (coloured if possible).

C Food

The poor were often hungry. They lived mainly on dark rye bread and oat cakes, and porridge made from peas, beans, and oatmeal. There was also home-made cheese, and sometimes a little salted pork. But there was hardly ever any fresh meat. To drink, they had ale or cider.

Kings and lords ate much more, and had more variety. They liked fish, beef, and venison, and drank huge amounts of wine. At a fifteenth century feast there would be dishes like roast peacock, swan, and stork. By that time, there were rich sauces made with spices from the Far East.

No-one had forks in the Middle Ages – they made do with knives, spoons, and their fingers. Peasants ate off wooden plates, and the rich used pewter. Table manners were crude. A fifteenth-century book says that in polite company you should not lick your plate clean, or spit too far!

Now try Exercise 16.3.

Source 16f

A beggar at a feast

Source 16d

A Norman feast

Source 16e

Cooking on a spit

Exercise 16.3

Read **Section C** and look at **Sources 16d**, **16e**, and **16f**.
What was a lord's feast like in the Middle Ages? What do the sources tell you about the following? (Write at least a sentence about each.)

a The food and how it was cooked.
b Plates, cups, knives, forks, spoons, etc.
c Servants.
d Beggars and animals.

D Education

Children were not forced by law to go to school, and most girls did not go at all. **Some** boys went to school with the village priest. For a small fee, he taught them to read, write, and do simple arithmetic. The boys had to sit on benches, often in the church porch, and learn their lessons by heart. (Look at source 16h.) Pupils who were badly behaved or lazy were flogged.

Rich men's sons went on to **grammar schools**, where they learned Latin, and nothing else. By the age of fourteen, they could read, write, and speak it as well as they could English.

Latin was the language of the church. The Mass and the Bible were in Latin. The books which the monks copied were in Latin. So were the chronicles which they wrote. All over Europe, educated men spoke and wrote to each other in Latin. Students travelled a long way to hear learned priests lecturing, in Latin, in the 'schools'. (We would call them universities.) In the twelfth century, English students crossed to the schools of Paris. By the year 1200, there were schools at Oxford, and at Cambridge soon after. (Read source 16g.)

Many rich men sent their daughters to school in nunneries. The nuns taught them to read and write, and to behave like ladies. They might learn a little French and Latin as well. By the year 1500, though, a lot of lords had private tutors for their daughters. At the end of the Middle Ages, many noble women were very fine scholars.

Now try Exercise 16.4.

Source 16g

There was a scholar from Oxford. His horse was as lean as a rake. And he wasn't fat himself. His cheeks were hollow, and he had a sad face. His coat was threadbare, for he had very little money. But he would rather have twenty books, bound in red and black, than any number of fine robes.

From Geoffrey Chaucer's *Canterbury Tales*. The scholar was a teacher in the university.

A schoolroom

Source 16h

A woman teaching reading. Many women in the middle ages could read better than their husbands.

Exercise 16.4

Answers do not always have to be right or wrong.

Sometimes, there is more than one answer to a question. Sometimes, two persons have different opinions, without one of them being wrong. It is possible to try to 'see both sides of a question'.

Try to 'see both sides of' this question (**Section D** on page 84 will help you.)

Was it sensible for grammar-school pupils to spend all their time learning Latin?

Think about the subjects which *you* study at school. Pupils in the Middle Ages missed all of them.

Write two paragraphs giving:

a Reasons why spending so much time on Latin was a **good** idea.
b Reasons why spending so much time on Latin was a **bad** idea.

E Health and sickness

For most men and women, life was hard. For many, it was short. A lot of children died young, and at fifty a man or woman was old. Lack of food was often the basic cause of sickness and death. But impure water and dirty houses with no proper drains played their part. When disease struck, death soon followed.

Only the rich could call in a doctor when they were ill. But doctors often did more harm than good. (They used to **bleed** patients to get rid of fever.) Their knowledge came mainly from the ancient **Greeks**. It had been passed on to **Arab** scholars in the Near East and Spain. From them, it reached the west. But this knowledge came only from books. No-one knew much about how the body really worked.

Doctors did know about **infectious** and **contagious** diseases. **Leprosy** was the most feared of them. Lepers were made to live apart, in 'lazar houses'. They had to wear special cloaks, and carry bells or clappers to warn that they were coming. They could not even go to church. In a way, this cruel treatment worked. By 1500, there were only a few lepers in England.

Monasteries and **hospitals** gave clean beds and decent food to some of the sick and old. And monks made medicines from the herbs they grew in their gardens. As a rule, though, fami-

A doctor in the Middle Ages making medicines.

Operating on a patient's head.

Source 16i

Some 'cures' from the Middle Ages

a A cure for leprosy. ***Make an ointment from unicorn's liver and the white of an egg.***
b A cure for smallpox. ***Wrap the patient in a red cloth. Hang red curtains at the windows and round the bed.***
c A headache cure. ***Make a mixture of leaves of green rue, mustard seed, and the white of an egg. Using a feather, smear it on the side of the head that is not sore.***

Source 16j

A stick which once belonged to St Curig is good for getting rid of lumps on the body. You are cured if you kneel before the stick and make a gift of a penny. A man with a lump once gave only a half-penny. The result was that only half his lump went down.

From a book about Wales written by a priest called Gerald in 1188.

lies looked after their own. Women kept 'cures' (part fact, part magic) among their recipes. But they, and most others, had more faith in prayers to the saints than in medicine.

Now try Exercises 16.5 and 16.6.

Exercise 16.5

Read **Section E** and **Sources 16i** and **16j**.
Write at least one sentence in answer to each of the questions.

a What was the doctors' **motive** for bleeding their patients?
b What was the **motive** for forcing lepers to live separate lives?
c What was the monks' **motive** for taking care of the old and sick? (If you are not sure, read the beginning of Chapter 4 again.)
d What do you think were the **motives** of the doctors, monks, and others who said that the 'cures' in **Source 16i** worked?
e What do you think might have been Gerald's **motive** (**Source 16j**) for telling the story about St. Curig's stick?

Exercise 16.6

Discuss in a group:

a the things you would have liked about living in the Middle Ages.
b the things you would have disliked.

Make a chart or wall display divided into two halves – good things and bad things. Draw pictures or cartoons for the display **or** write short pieces in your own words.

17 Women in the Middle Ages

A A woman's place...

It was a man's world. Girls obeyed their fathers before marriage, and their husbands after. If they did not, they were beaten. Even the church said that men had a right to beat their wives. Most villages had a ducking stool for 'scolds' – women who nagged their husbands.

Some women lived without men. Ladies whose husbands were at the wars had to look after the estates. All the servants and tenants – men and women – had to take orders from them. **Widows** had to manage alone. Most widows were poor, and many must have starved. But rich merchants' widows were well off. And craftsmen's widows got help from the guilds.

Many rich men's daughters became **nuns**. (Their fathers had to make a gift of money when they entered the convent.) The abbess was often the daughter of a lord. Nuns' main work was to teach the daughters of good families how to behave like ladies, and how to read and write. The only men allowed in convents were the priests who came to say Mass.

Men were supposed to be the bosses. This did not stop some women from getting their own way. And in the songs and stories of the Middle Ages, women had a very high place. Knights were supposed to fight for their ladies, and defend them from all dangers, such as dragons!

Now try Exercise 17.1.

A woman making her confession to a priest.

Source 17a

When you are walking in the street, keep your head still and look straight ahead. Fix your eyes on the ground about 20 yards in front of you. Do not look up, or glance at any men or women. Do not laugh. Do not stop to speak to anyone in the street.

Instructions for his young wife written by Goodman of Paris in the fourteenth century.

Exercise 17.1

Read **Section A** and **Source 17a**.
Write 'True' or 'False' after each sentence.

a The church said that women were equal to their husbands. _____

b Women who nagged their husbands were punished in public. _____

c All widows were very poor. _____

d Male servants wouldn't take orders from women. _____

e Only rich men's daughters became nuns. _____

f Nuns were able to read and write. _____

g Knights were expected to defend their ladies. _____

h Goodman of Paris (**Source 17a**) expected his wife to appear shy and modest. _____

i Goodman did not mind if his wife chatted to her friends. _____

j Goodman himself probably did not speak to people in the streets. _____

© Oxford University Press

B Marriage

Most girls married young – at fifteen or sixteen, or younger. They married the men their fathers chose. For marriage, at least to the rich, was business. Only the really poor married for love.

It cost a man money to feed and clothe a daughter. When she got married, her husband took on the job of keeping her. So her father paid the bridegroom some money or gave him a present. This was the **dowry**. All but the very poor paid dowries. Tradesmen might give some furniture and cooking pots. Kings and great lords paid vast sums.

A marriage, and the payment of a dowry, was a deal between two families. If the fathers were kings, it might be part of a peace treaty. If they were merchants, it was a piece of business. The young people's wishes had nothing to do with it.

Heiresses were special. They were girls who had no brothers. When their fathers died, they (and their husbands) got the land or money. Many men dreamed of marrying a rich heiress. To a king, marrying an heiress was as good as winning a war. Henry II of England became ruler of all of south-west France when he married Eleanor of Aquitaine.

Now try Exercise 17.2.

The poet Chaucer wrote about the Wealthy Wife of Bath. She had been married five times and was looking for a sixth husband.

Exercise 17.2

Read **Section B**.
Use your own words to write brief notes about the following:

a The age at which girls married.
b Choice of husband.
c Dowries.
   i What was a dowry?
   ii Which classes of people paid dowries?
   iii Why were dowries paid?
d Marriage was a deal or treaty.
e Heiresses.

Weddings in the Middle Ages took place at the church door, not in the church.

C Women's Work

Married women had a lot of children, but about half of them died young. Not even the rich were spared the pain and sadness of bearing children who lived only a year or two. Often the mothers themselves died in childbirth.

Rich ladies had servants to do the housework and look after the children. The ladies gave orders to the servants and kept the accounts. They had time to talk, read, and write letters. Most of them did some weaving or embroidery.

Craftsmen's wives had serving girls to help run the house. But they had to cook and see to the children themselves. They also served in the shop, and made sure the apprentices kept out of mischief. They had no time to spare.

Peasant women had the hardest life of all. They had to cook, clean, care for the children, and help their husbands in the fields. On top of that, they would spin yarn and make cheese to sell in the market. Most of the time they must have been cold, wet, hungry, and tired. Not many lived much beyond the age of thirty.

Now try Exercise 17.3.

A peasant woman cooking a meal for her children.

Source 17b

The poorest folk are the widows with children. The landlords keep putting their rent up. The money they make by spinning has to be spent on rent, or on milk and oatmeal for the hungry children. These women are often miserable with hunger and cold. They get up before dawn to card and comb the wool, to wash and scrub and mend, and wind yarn.

From *Piers Ploughman*, written by William Langland in about 1380.

Source 17c

I saw a poor man and his wife ploughing. She had a short coat, with a sheet on top to keep out the weather. Her feet were bare. At the end of the field was a basket, with a little child in it, wrapped in rags. Two others, about two years old, stood beside it. They were all crying in misery.

From *Pierce the Ploughman's Crede*, written in the 1390s.

Exercise 17.3

Read **Section C** and **Sources 17b** and **17c**.
Write down at least five **reasons** why peasant women had a hard and miserable life.

Source 17d

When I was in Norwich this week, I called at my mother's. While I was there Mr Wrothe came in. He saw our daughter, who was with me, and said she was a fine-looking girl. My mother asked him if he could find her a good husband. He said that he knew a young man from a good family, who has an income of £200 a year. He is eighteen years old. What do you think about the idea? My mother thinks that if we wait any longer we will have to pay a bigger dowry.

A letter from Margaret Paston to her husband in 1462.

Source 17e

Exercise 17.4

Read **Source 17d**, then answer the questions in sentences.

a Where did Mrs Paston's mother live?
d What was Mr Wrothe's **opinion** of Mrs Paston's daughter?
c Which *three* **facts** about the young man did Mr Wrothe mention?
d What was Mrs Paston's mother's **opinion** about the marriage?
e Did Mrs Paston say what her opinion was?
f Which *two* people were not asked for their opinions?

Source 17f

There once was a merchant, who had so much money that people thought he must be wise. His wife was beautiful and liked company. They were always having visitors at their house. Now the wife loved fine clothes and ornaments. The merchant liked her to be well dressed, for it showed how rich he was. But he had to pay the bills!

From one of the stories in Geoffrey Chaucer's *Canterbury Tales*, written in about 1390.

Exercise 17.5

Look at **Source 17e** and read **Source 17f**.
Answer questions **a** to **f** in sentences, and question **g** in a paragraph.

a Who wrote **Source 17f**, and when?
b Is **Source 17f** fact or fiction? (Look at **Source 3g** on page 18 if you are not sure.)
c What does **Source 17f** tell us about the merchant's wife?
d Where does **Source 17e** come from?
e What does **Source 17e** tell us about the rich lady?
f Could the lady in **Source 17e** have been the same person as the lady in **Source 17f**?
g How much do **Sources 17e** and **17f** tell us about rich ladies in the late Middle Ages? (Which things do they tell us about, and which things do they not tell us about?)

This brass engraving from a tomb in Isleham church, Cambridge shows a rich lady dressed in the style of about 1485.

18 Crime and Punishment

A Sheriffs, Judges, and Juries

England had no police force in the Middle Ages. Instead, all the peasants had to join a **tithing**. This was a group of men who made sure that their neighbours behaved. If there was a crime, the tithing had to say who had done it. If they did not, they were all punished.

Also, when a crime took place, all the men in a town or village had to join the **hue and cry**. This meant that they were supposed to rush out and chase the suspect. If they caught him, they handed him over to the sheriff. Of course, the suspect often got away.

The **sheriff** was the king's man in each county. One of his jobs was to catch criminals and put them in prison. He kept them there until the king's **judges** arrived on their tour of the country.

The judges were told what crimes had taken place. Then a **jury** said who had committed the crimes, if they knew. If the accused man or woman confessed, he or she was sentenced. If not, he or she went to **trial by ordeal**. (See Section B).

Now try Exercise 18.1.

Source 18a

Hue and Cry

At least four armed men in each village have to keep watch all night. When a stranger passes through, they must arrest him. If they think he is not honest, they have to hand him over to the sheriff. If the stranger runs away, they must raise the hue and cry. All the men of the village should then join in the chase until the suspect is caught.

A law passed by King Henry III in 1242.

The court of king's bench in the fifteenth century. Try to find the five judges, the clerks, the ushers with their sticks, the lawyers, and the prisoners.

Source **18b**

Juries

Twelve men from each district must come before the judges. They must say whether any man in their area is a robber, or murderer, or thief. If a man is accused, and says he is not guilty, there must be a trial by ordeal.

A law passed by King Henry II in 1166.

Exercise 18.1

Read **Section A** and **Sources 18a** and **18b**.
Write notes on keeping law and order in the Middle Ages.
Use your own words.

a Say what a tithing was.
b Say what hue and cry meant. (Read **Source 18a**.)
c Say what a sheriff did.
d Say what a jury did. (Use **Source 18b**.)

B Trial by Ordeal and Trial by Combat

Trial by ordeal was the way of judging an accused person. The idea was that God would decide who was guilty and who was innocent. So the man or woman had to take a test. The result would show God's verdict. If God, through the ordeal, said 'guilty', the accused was punished.

In **ordeal by fire**, the accused had to walk a few paces, carrying a piece of red-hot iron in the palm of his or her hand. The hand was burned, so it was

Trial by ordeal.

Trial by combat

bandaged. After three days, the judges took off the bandage and looked at the burned hand. If it was starting to heal, the person was innocent. If it was not healing, he was guilty.

Ordeal by water was simpler. The accused was thrown into a pond. If he sank, he was innocent. (If he was lucky he was fished out before he drowned.) If he floated, he was guilty.

In **trial by combat**, the man who brought the charge had to fight the person he accused. The first one to be knocked down had to admit he was in the wrong. Women and children could hire 'champions' to fight for them.

By the year 1300, trial by ordeal had been given up. Instead, a jury decided whether the accused was guilty or not. Trial by combat lasted a little longer. But it too has been abolished. A thief cannot now offer to fight his accuser!

Now try Exercises 18.2 and 18.3.

C Punishments

You could be hanged for all sorts of crimes in the Middle Ages. But not all criminals were put to death. Many had to pay fines. A law passed by King Henry II in 1176 said that thieves had to have a hand and a foot cut off. Then they had to go into exile (leave England for ever). The king got all their money and goods.

Sheriffs' prisons were mainly for persons waiting to be tried. There were **dungeons** in lords' castles, of course. Powerful lords kept their enemies locked up for years. The stocks, pillory, and ducking-stool were for small-scale crime. Traders who cheated in the market would get a spell in the pillory. It taught them a lesson and warned other traders. And it was cheap entertainment for the public.

Exercise 18.2

Read **Section B. Written sources** tell us what happened in trial by ordeal and trial by combat. But there are very few **pictures** from the Middle Ages.

How might pictures have helped us?

Write down some questions which you could have answered if there had been pictures. (The cartoon might give you some ideas.)

Exercise 18.3

a Before Henry II's time, each **lord** had his own court. The lord acted as judge. He could hang the peasants, or make them pay fines. Henry II changed this. He said the courts were under the king's control. He sent his judges round England to hear cases.

Suggest a reason why this change was popular with the common people.

b In the thirteenth century, trial by ordeal was stopped. Instead, **juries** decided whether accused persons were guilty.

Suggest a reason why this was a change for the better.

c Which people might have been sorry to see the end of trial by combat, and why?

A ducking stool, which was often used for punishing women who had done wrong.

The Legend of Robin Hood

Men who had done wrong, but did not turn up in court, were condemned as **outlaws**. For the rest of their lives, they had no rights. It was not a crime to kill them, or steal from them. Many outlaws fled to the **forests**. These were partly wooded places where only the king could hunt. It was a crime for anyone else to kill deer there. Outlaws in the forests robbed travellers and killed the deer.

The most famous outlaws are **Robin Hood** and his 'merry men'. The story is a legend, but some things in it are true. There was a forest called Sherwood. There was a sheriff of Nottingham. In about 1230, in Yorkshire, there was even an outlaw called **Robert Hood**.

Now try Exercises 18.4 and 18.5

This picture was painted in about 1840. It shows Robin Hood and his men dining with the king in Sherwood Forest. The ballads say that this happened, but they do not say which king it was. King Edward II did pass through **Sherwood Forest** in 1323. Perhaps he met Robin Hood then.

Source 18c

The story told in the ballads written in the fifteenth century

Robin Hood was an outlaw. Little John and Will Scarlett were members of his band. Robin and the 'merry men' lived in Sherwood Forest and Barnsdale in Yorkshire. They dressed in Lincoln green. They were good archers, and their main food was the king's deer. Their enemies were the sheriff of Nottingham and the Abbot of St Mary's in York. They robbed rich travellers, but took nothing from the poor.

Robin Hood – drawn in 1795.

An archer – drawn in the Middle Ages.

Source 18d

The story as it is told today

Robin Hood was the leader of a band of outlaws. Among his 'merry men' were Little John, Will Scarlett, and Friar Tuck. His girl-friend was called Maid Marion. Robin and the outlaws lived in Sherwood Forest. They dressed in Lincoln green. They were expert archers, and lived by killing the king's deer. Their great enemy was the sheriff of Nottingham. They robbed the rich, and gave money to the poor.

Exercise 18.4

Read **Section C** and **Sources 18c** and **18d**.
How has the legend of Robin Hood changed between the fifteenth century (Source 18c) and today (Source 18d)?
Write notes, answering the questions below.

a What changes have taken place in the **people** in the legend? Which persons have stayed the same? Which persons have been added? Which persons have dropped out?
b Do the events happen in the same **place**? Have there been any changes?
c Have there been changes in the outlaws' **dress** and **food**?
d Have there been any changes in the **events** – the things the outlaws did?

Exercise 18.5

Most legends have some truth in them. We can study legends, and find out which things **are** true, which things **may be** true, and which things **are probably not** true.
How much of the Robin Hood story is **true**, and how much is **fiction**?
Read **Section C** and **Sources 18c** and **18d** again.
Note down the answers to these questions, then discuss your answers in a group:

a Which things in the Robin Hood story are **true**?
(Use these words as a guide: outlaws, forests, Sherwood, sheriff of Nottingham, deer, robbery.)
b Was there ever a real Robin (or Robert) Hood, and did he live in the right place? (Look at the map.)
c Which things in the story (**Source 18d**) do you think are **fiction**?

Your group should make a chart or wall display with drawings, a map, and written pieces. It should show which things in the story are true, which are fiction, and which you are not sure about.

Criteria grid

Attainment target 1: Knowledge and understanding of history

a	Historical Knowledge	1.1 2.1 3.3 4.2 5.1 6.1 7.1 8.2 9.2 10.2 11.1 12.1 13.1 14.1 15.3 16.2 17.1 18.3	
		1.2 2.3 4.3 5.3 6.3 7.2 8.3 9.3 11.2 13.4 14.3 15.4 17.3	
b	Concepts & terminology	1.3 4.2 5.1 6.2 10.1 12.3 14.2 17.2 18.1	
c	Chronology;		
	i Dates & sequence	2.2 **8.1** 10.2 13.1	
	ii Conventions (e.g. centuries)	**3.2** **7.3** 9.1 10.5 15.3	
d	Cause & consequence	**3.5** **5.3** 8.3 11.2 12.4 15.4 17.3	
e	Motivation	1.1 **5.4** 7.2 13.4 16.5	
f	Continuity & change	2.5 4.3 6.3 10.4 12.1 14.3 15.3 16.2 18.3	
g	Different features of situations*	2.6 **4.5** 5.6 7.5 8.4 9.5 13.5 15.2 16.6 17.4 18.3	

Attainment target 2: Interpretations of history

a	Distinguishing fact & fiction	3.1 9.4 17.5 18.5
b	Different versions of events & topics	1.5 3.1 8.4 10.3 11.1 12.2 13.5 18.4
c	Recognizing fact & opinion	**2.4** 3.4 11.3 14.4
d	Different interpretations	**6.4** 7.4 8.5 11.3 12.5 13.3 **16.4**
e	Reasons for different interpretations	**7.4** 8.5 13.3

Attainment target 3: The use of historical sources

a	Acquiring information	1.1 2.1 3.3 4.1 5.2 6.1 7.1 8.2 9.3 10.2 11.5 12.1 13.1 14.1 15.1 16.3 17.3
b	Sources - authorship & dates	**1.4** 3.1 5.5 6.5 14.5 15.5
c	Primary & secondary sources	**4.4** 5.5 12.4 14.5
d	Making deductions from sources	7.6 8.6 11.4 13.2 17.5
e	Using different kinds of source	1.5 2.3 4.1 7.1 8.2 9.5 11.5 12.1 13.5 14.1 15.3 16.2 17.1
f	Value and reliability of evidence	**6.5** 8.6 9.2 14.5 15.5 16.1 18.2

* Includes attitudes & points of view of participants in situations & events.